# Style & Simplicity

## An A to Z Guide to Living a More Beautiful Life

TED KENNEDY WATSON

*Sterling Signature*
NEW YORK

Sterling Signature
NEW YORK

An Imprint of Sterling Publishing
387 Park Avenue South
New York, NY 10016

ISBN 978-1-4549-0724-4

Distributed in Canada by Sterling Publishing
c/o Canadian Manda Group, 165 Dufferin Street
Toronto, Ontario, Canada M6K 3H6
Distributed in the United Kingdom by
GMC Distribution Services
Castle Place, 166 High Street, Lewes,
East Sussex, England BN7 1XU
Distributed in Australia by Capricorn Link (Australia) Pty. Ltd.
P.O. Box 704, Windsor, NSW 2756, Australia

Design by Brent Whiting and Ted Kennedy Watson

For information about custom editions, special sales,
and premium and corporate purchases, please contact
Sterling Special Sales at 800-805-5489 or
specialsales@sterlingpublishing.com.

Manufactured in China

10 9 8 7 6 5 4 3 2 1

www.sterlingpublishing.com

# Contents

TO MY FATHER, KENNEDY WATSON, who died when he was sixty-one years old and who was an extraordinary being with an amazing thirst for life. Losing him so early taught me to cherish each day and to relish each minute. His positive outlook and good humor are both things I try to incorporate into every moment in his honor.

TO MY HUSBAND, MISTER SIVE, whose creativity and kindness inspire me daily—it has always been we, not I, which makes everything so much sweeter. Thank you for more than twenty-five years of traveling this beautiful adventure called life together.

# Foreword

ONE OF THE THINGS I LOVE about my work is the opportunity it gives me to travel, and one of the things I love most about traveling is that open space between flights—a space I like to fill in search of discovery; a space in which a chance encounter might present itself. A few years ago in Seattle, with only an hour to spare, I wandered into a magical little shop a block off the pulsating and lively waterfront. Immediately upon entering I fell—in an Alice-in-Wonderland kind of way—into a world of seduction and sensory experience. Cleverly arranged, on shelf, after shelf, after shelf, were bibelots, *objets d'art* and curios from around the world as well as from right around the corner. Each one seemed to call out to be picked up, read about, inhaled, and experienced. In delighted reverie, I read my way along the shelves, from one little note to another. These were not just any notes; they were personal, handwritten, calligraphic notes that either described the origins of items, their previous provenances, or a novel way in which to use something mundane. "The perfect birthday gift" said one note, "One-of-a-kind" said another, and "A flea market find!" said yet one more. As if that were not enough, each item was lovingly polished to absolute, shiny perfection. Needless to say, my heart skipped several beats. I remember thinking, "This is not simply a gift shop, but a shop that is a gift." A gift from someone who had brought his treasures and special finds home with a very clear intention: to share with a shopper like me, or rather the lucky shopper who found her way to Ted Kennedy Watson.

I'm not sure how long I wandered, as I lost track of time the moment I entered the shop. Finally, when I did look up, standing behind the counter was a cheerful, smiling man (who I suspected had been watching me wander all along). Having inherited my Irish father's gift for talking—rarely, am I at a loss for words—in this remarkable shop all I could muster was, "This place is amazing." Chuckling like Santa Claus, Ted introduced himself. I think he knew right then that he had met a kindred soul, a like-minded lover of beauty, a devotee of shopping "finds." As I unloaded my armful of eclectic curiosities onto his glass-topped counter, we fell into a seamless conversation until I suddenly remembered, "My plane!"

Arriving home, I saw my "TKW" package and tore right into it. Not only was it a delight to open, but each and every purchase had been wrapped and tied with bows! To my further amazement, there were things included that I hadn't even purchased. And attached to those things were those wonderful calligraphic notes, this time saying things like "I thought you might appreciate this." Right then I realized that Ted had managed to wrap up and ship his special magic into my home.

Ted Kennedy Watson, the store, makes so apparent what is all too rare in retail today . . . soul, born from its proprietor. Ted Kennedy Watson, the man, makes so apparent what is also rare in people—someone who not only loves what he is doing, but also does it with love. There is no substitute for Ted's discerning eye, no match for his talent, and no replacement for his hard work. Ted's specific kind of caring grows out of a generosity and a gracious way of being in the world. Whether I'm visiting his store—my first stop off the plane in Seattle—or reading his engaging stories on his blog, Ted engenders connection. He opens our eyes and our hearts, like he opened mine.

And now here, in his first book, Ted has again grabbed my full attention as he shares the secrets of his favorite things from A to Z. So if Seattle isn't on your agenda soon, you can now cozy up at home in your favorite chair and let the beauty of Ted Kennedy Watson unfold.

—*Barbara Barry*

# Introduction

**AS I SIT AT THE DESK IN OUR STUDY,** with my ever-present favorite green glass of sparkling water with lemon next to me, I am very much aware of what creature comforts and simple luxuries mean to me. For as long as I can remember, the minute details of life have been incredibly important to me. My goal in writing this book is to share with you many of those details and observations so that you may start, or continue, to see them in your own world and relish in them, too. The details in my everyday life are no more special than those in anyone else's, but by sharing mine with you, my hope is that you begin to see them in yours. Seeing the small details requires slowing down a bit and being aware of your surroundings.

This book is meant to be a guide, an A to Z of specific "things" I see in my day-to-day life and how I have interpreted them in different ways. From my early years as a design showroom owner and as an artist representative, to my current role as a shopkeeper, design and style blogger, and entertainer, my days have been filled with the quest for stylish living and for getting the very best out of each moment. I would love to share with you some of the tips, secrets, and ideas that I have used with much happy success. My hope is that I can encourage you, too, to look at these very same things and perhaps interpret them in a different, singular light of your own—snapshots of a moment, you might say. By breaking items down into a singular quality, we slow down and make ourselves more aware of our surroundings and become present in the moment. This book is really all about the small details that make our daily lives rich. Personal style is truly just that— personal style. It is your style that develops over time. My purpose is not to have you adopt mine, but for you to expand upon, or find, your own personal style.

Your home is your personal oasis. My hope is that by showing you my world, it will get your mind churning with ideas. This book is filled with components that I use at my shops and homes to make them comfortable, visually rich, and personal. Pulled together, they create my personal style. Choose one or many, mix and match, using what you think helps define your style. There really is no right or wrong. Your home should bring you joy and create comfort. After all, it is your life and your home, which should reflect your taste and make you incredibly happy.

Living creatively is not meant to be about money; rather, it is about being creative with the choices that present themselves to you during the day. It is about being aware of your options and how you choose to view them. I have known some uber-creative souls with beautifully creative lives who live on very little. And I have known folks who have made a good deal of dough but have very little creativity or interest in their lives. It is about the choices that are made each moment and how you decide to view them. I hope what is being presented in the following pages speaks to everyone, and helps make you aware of all the glorious details swirling around in your world.

On my daily blog, www.TedKennedyWatson.com, I share recipes, table settings, shop vignettes, and all the things I enjoy or that inspire me. I have always been of the mind-set that if a person can perform a small list of things really well, then that can be parlayed into doing many things well, like roasting a simple chicken, whipping up a martini, setting a creative table for dinner, making an easy vinaigrette, or putting together a stylish flower arrangement. Master these first, and then add your own spin and variation on them.

There are two goals I want to achieve with this book: (1) to fill it with ideas, inspirations, quotes, and resources—a workbook of sorts—and (2) for it to be something that can be given as a gift to spark creativity. My hope with this list of A to Z things to live a beautiful life is that it be a starting point for beginning your own list. My list has things and experiences that fill my life each day with a tremendous amount of joy. So often I feel that it is the big moments in life which are given great emphasis, but the small moments are equally, if not more, important—moments such as enjoying the unfurling of a tulip petal or catching the scent of a candle when you enter a room. Living in the moment, not in preparation for the moment, is my prevailing thought.

My list is a starting point to get your mind racing with what is important in your life. While many of the things on my list are just things, they all make me aware and more appreciative of my life, be it a recipe I share and make for a dinner or a big bunch of peonies I arrange to be enjoyed when guests arrive. My list could have been four times as long; I kept it down to experiences that fill my days with tremendous beauty and joy—two qualities I am always looking to incorporate into every aspect of my daily life.

I hope you enjoy the words I have written and the photos I have taken, for they have been a lovely part of my journey to create this book for you. My feeling has always been that we have this one life to live, so let's live it as exquisitely as we can.

—*Ted Kennedy Watson*

ONE OF THE EASIEST WAYS to make your home truly self-expressive is to fill it with artwork you love and have collected over time. Very few things are more telling of someone's personality than the art they have in their home. Collecting and acquiring art can be intimidating, but it doesn't have to be. Think outside the box and don't assume the only place to buy art is at a gallery. Art is such a personal thing. Buy what stirs an emotion. I think people worry too much about whether their art will be liked by others. Buy what you love, as *you* are the one who will be living with it each day. Here are some tips for starting your collection:

- Many art schools have auctions where students sell their work. Research some schools near you and attend one. It's a great way to support the arts and to obtain great, fresh artwork at reasonable prices.

- Lots of retail shops, like mine, carry a variety of art, which makes the experience of shopping for a piece far less intimidating.

- Many beginning artists have shows in studio spaces they share with other artists. Attend a studio show and add to your collection—you will also be helping a novice artist.

- Be on the lookout when you travel. Buying art on vacation is a wonderful way to remember a trip. We purchased one of our very first pieces in New York from an artist on the street. To this day, it is still one of our favorites. We have kept in touch with the artist over the years and have added other pieces to our collection from shows in which she has exhibited.

- Artwork is not only for the walls. Look at sculptures, ephemera, pottery, even things from nature like a piece of bark—whatever catches your eye.

# Adirondack Chairs

ADIRONDACK CHAIRS JUST SHOUT, "Come relax in me!" and are, in my opinion, the best chair choice for unwinding outside with a book—or a cocktail. The first Adirondack chairs, called Westport chairs, were named after the town of Westport, New York, on the edge of Lake Champlain, close to the Adirondack Mountains. Choose a color that makes you happy. They are now offered in many colorways, but I almost always prefer classic white. Either solo or placed together in a row, Adirondack chairs speak of a slower time.

No texting or tweeting allowed!

# Apples

BAGS OF APPLES from the grocery store can be a great and inexpensive decorating tool, if you buy them at the right time. For this table setting pictured, I had originally planned to set it outside using melamine John Derian apple plates we had recently acquired, in addition to some flour sack towels with an apple motif. I love using dish towels as napkins for outside or messy meals. Red flowers were nowhere to be found, so I quickly ran to the grocer and found a few bags of apples. I scattered a variety of apples about, mixing in green and red glass votive candleholders to play off the colors of the apples. Finally, red-handled Laguiole flatware tied it all together. One truism I have discovered in my career is that sometimes not finding what we had first planned, such as red flowers in this case, forces us to think creatively—often giving a result that turns out better than what we had originally envisioned.

{ *Nothing is worth more than this day.* }
— *Johann Wolfgang von Goethe*

# Antique Malls

ANTIQUE MALLS ARE ONE OF MY FAVORITE sources for finding great vintage treasures. Filled with groupings of individual vendors who have their own spaces and sell their own wares within the mall, they are great places to find a vast variety of vintage goods in a short amount of time. Oil paintings, glassware, lamps, ephemera—you name it—are treasures just waiting to be snapped up. Antique malls are also the perfect places to begin a collection, as there is such a large selection of similar or "like" goods to choose from. Pacific Galleries in Seattle; Stars Antique Malls in Portland, Oregon; and Alfies Antique Market in London, England, are a few of my very favorites. Do a quick Google search and you can easily find one near you. Have fun starting a collection!

*Decorating is not about making stage sets; it's not about making pretty pictures for magazines; it's really about creating a quality of life, a beauty that nourishes the soul.*

—Albert Hadley

ALABASTER LAMPS HAVE AN OLD WORLD look and vibe which many rooms could benefit from. The vintage models are often Italian-made, and can be picked up at antique stores and flea markets. I find it safest to have all vintage lamps rewired—many lighting shops can do the job. If you don't find a shade to your liking, an exposed old-school Edison bulb looks just great and is what we use at my shops quite often. The warm glow of the Edison bulb against the alabaster evokes the feeling of an earlier, simpler time.

# Alabaster Lamps

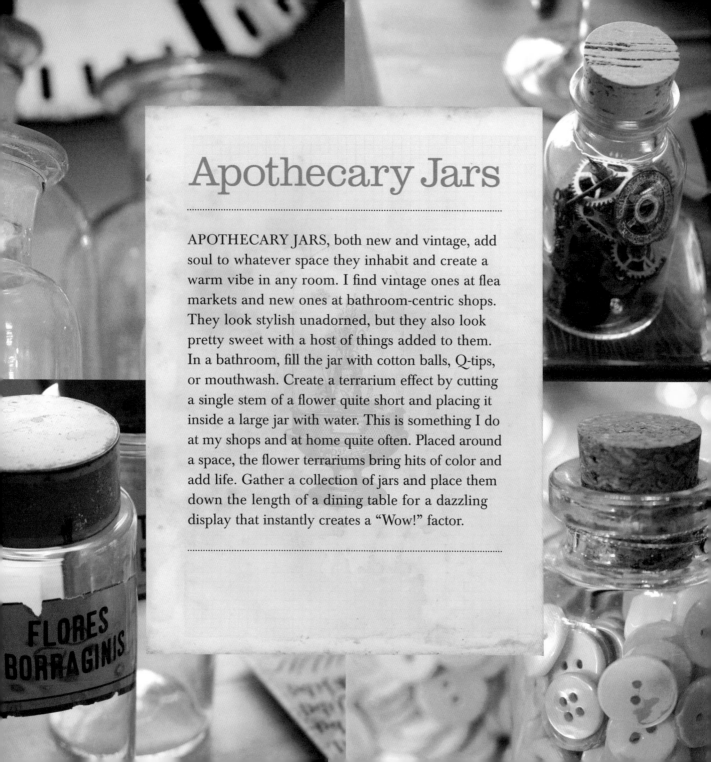

# Apothecary Jars

APOTHECARY JARS, both new and vintage, add soul to whatever space they inhabit and create a warm vibe in any room. I find vintage ones at flea markets and new ones at bathroom-centric shops. They look stylish unadorned, but they also look pretty sweet with a host of things added to them. In a bathroom, fill the jar with cotton balls, Q-tips, or mouthwash. Create a terrarium effect by cutting a single stem of a flower quite short and placing it inside a large jar with water. This is something I do at my shops and at home quite often. Placed around a space, the flower terrariums bring hits of color and add life. Gather a collection of jars and place them down the length of a dining table for a dazzling display that instantly creates a "Wow!" factor.

# Asparagus

THIS BOOK AIMS TO SHOW, through example, how to look at certain things differently and how to see them through a creative eye. I often replicate in my own home many of the display ideas we create at my shops. One example is asparagus. While amazing to eat, asparagus is also quite beautiful to look at. They look like stems of flowers, and I use them as I would any type of flower. Take several bunches and place each one in a drinking glass. Line the glasses up and down your dining table or mantel. Many kinds of produce, like kale and cabbage, can make creative, lovely table settings or arrangements.

While amazing to eat, asparagus is also quite beautiful to look at.

# Basil

BASIL IS A HEARTY, fragrant herb that works beautifully in cooking, but also can be used in place of flowers and works quite nicely in big bunches in simple containers set about. The intoxicating scent will fill your room. You can find fresh basil that is rooted in cello bags at your grocer in the produce aisle. These work nicely, placed in your favorite glass on the kitchen counter, adding a hit of color and scent to your kitchen. For the simplest of salads, try tearing basil leaves over sliced tomatoes and mozzarella. Add a few pinches of salt and a few glugs of olive oil and you have a quick and easy caprese salad that will make you, or your guests, think of summer any time of the year.

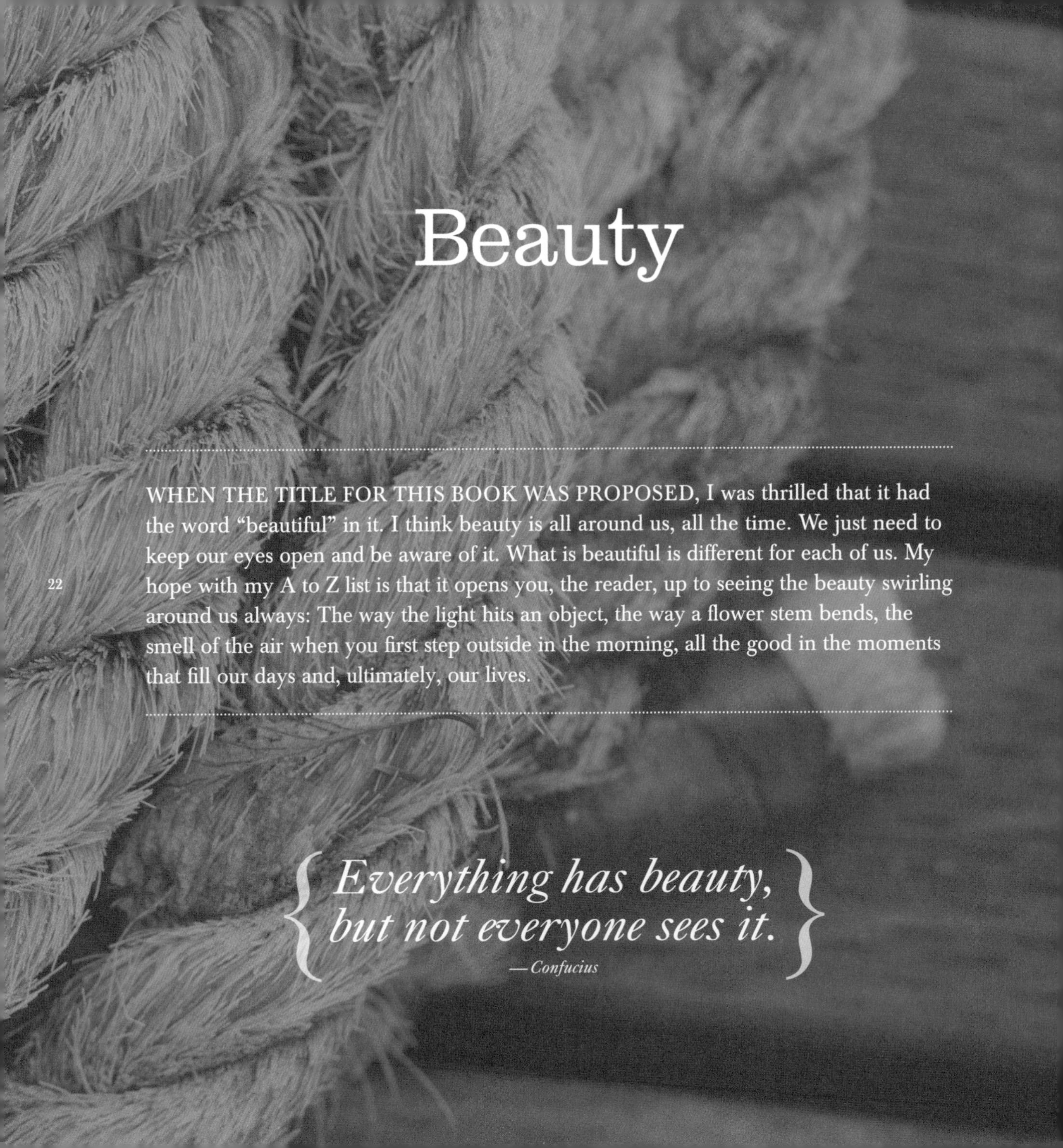

# Beauty

WHEN THE TITLE FOR THIS BOOK WAS PROPOSED, I was thrilled that it had the word "beautiful" in it. I think beauty is all around us, all the time. We just need to keep our eyes open and be aware of it. What is beautiful is different for each of us. My hope with my A to Z list is that it opens you, the reader, up to seeing the beauty swirling around us always: The way the light hits an object, the way a flower stem bends, the smell of the air when you first step outside in the morning, all the good in the moments that fill our days and, ultimately, our lives.

{ *Everything has beauty,*
*but not everyone sees it.* }
— *Confucius*

# Bread

GOOD BREAD MAKES FOR A SWELL GIFT. Many mail-order food sites now offer bread in their lineups. Two favorites of mine are Poilâne from Paris and Eli Zabar from New York. Like so many things nowadays, good breads are available in many options at grocery stores. The price difference between a mediocre loaf and an exceptional one is not always large, so I say, skimp in another area but treat yourself to good bread. If the loaf starts to harden before you have finished it, cut up the remaining portion into cubes to make croutons or put them into a food processor and transform into bread crumbs. You can also cut the leftover bread into slices and bake in the oven with a bit of olive oil for tasty crostini. For a simple bread salad to have for a tasty lunch, tear up stale bread into a bowl and add good extra virgin olive oil, salt, and pepper. Slice a couple of ripe tomatoes and mix everything together.

## ☞ TED'S TIP

Make extras to give to a neighbor the next time you are baking. The gift of homemade food is a gracious act.

BRANCHES ARE A LOVELY way to add a little nature to a room for some visual interest. I incorporate them into some of my displays at the shops, but they also look pretty weaved into a place in the home, too. Look for branches that have character and maybe a bit of lichen or moss on them. You are bringing nature inside, so be picky when choosing. Whether in a vase, used as a flower substitute, or draped over the top of a bookcase, branches add an earthiness to any room.

# Branches

# Ball Jars

FAVORED IN THE 1940s AND 1950s, vintage ball jars have become popular items to collect over the years. Most impressive about ball jars is how versatile they are. My friend Rita Konig has a mismatched, found set that she leaves out on her kitchen counter, in which she stores her sugar, flour, and other kitchen staples. Fill them with odd, matching bits of things, like buttons, to make practical art pieces out of storage. You not only get to display your collection of buttons in plain sight, but they are also neatly organized. Ball jars also look great when they are empty and lined up on a shelf, giving a sculptural hit to the space.

# Brie

*Baked Brie is one of those things that I associate with the 1980s, but, like all good things, it has made a comeback. When we whip this up to serve at a party, it's always the first thing to go—always. The best part is that it is the easiest thing to make! The recipe is really more about assembling than cooking, which always rates high in my book.*

## BAKED BRIE

1 Turn oven to 350 degrees to preheat while you assemble the ingredients.

2 Thaw one puff pastry sheet, following the instructions on the box. (I am a big fan of Pepperidge Farm, which is what I typically find at our grocer, but any brand is fine.)

3 Unfold the pastry sheets. As these are usually folded into thirds, cut one third off, and set aside for later.

4 Take a full, small package of Brie, open it, and cover the entire top in fig jam.

5 Moving carefully and quickly, flip the Brie over and onto the pastry sheet, so that the jam is now on the bottom.

6 Fold the sides of the pastry sheet up and over the Brie, encasing the entire concoction.

7 Flip the pastry over onto a baking sheet, preferably one lined with parchment paper.

8 Press out a few decorative images into the reserved third of the pastry sheet using a cookie cutter, or use a sharp knife to make a fun and creative motif.

9 Add the images to the top of the pastry.

10 Crack an egg into a bowl and add a splash of water to make an egg wash, and beat together.

11 Brush the egg mixture over the top and sides of the pastry; this will help it to brown.

12 Bake for 20 to 30 minutes, until puffy and golden brown. Let the pastry sit for a bit before serving, so the cheese is not too hot. It is best warm, but room temperature is fine as well. It's that easy. If you prefer another jam, then go for it. (Fig jam, however, has an earthiness that I like.)

# Baskets

BASKETS ARE THE KIND OF ITEMS that can simplify and beautify your life tremendously. Old or new, baskets are both pretty to look at and utilitarian to use. Whether in the kitchen holding lemons or onions or in the bathroom holding excess toiletries, baskets warm up any space by being just what they are. We use baskets at the shops to hold wrapping paper and ribbon. They are so pretty filled up. This is easy to replicate at home, too, using one as a holder of things big and small, important or not.

# Beeswax Candles

THEIR SCENT, NATURAL COLOR, and honeycomb pattern—these are just a few things I adore about beeswax candles. They have been a staple at my shops since day one. The softness of the wax makes them a great candle option when you are using taper holders, as beeswax is pliable, making it easy to form-fit into the openings. Beeswax candles have been used for their effective, aromatic burning properties since ancient Roman times. Their honeycomb pattern illuminates ever so slightly when lit, while a slightly sweet scent fills the air.

☞ TED'S TIP

Light a candle the minute you walk in the door in the evening.

BIRDS ARE SUCH GRACEFUL AND BEAUTIFUL CREATURES. I chose birds for my A to Z list because they are so industrious. If you've ever had the good fortune of watching a bird build a nest, you will understand what I mean. Stick by stick, piece by piece, it adds to its home. I am always amazed how a bird will fly in with a piece of stick and then fly right back out with it, as if to say, "Nope, that is just not right here." I feel  that creating our own nest-homes should be treated in very much the same way—piece by piece, only keeping what really resonates with us. If you fill your home that way, it will envelop you and others. You will be so excited to arrive home each evening after work. If something does not work, donate it. Surrounding yourself with only the things you truly love will make for one very special home.

Birds

bird

# Bitters

BITTERS HAVE BECOME ALL THE RAGE in the last few years. I don't really think of bitters as trendy, as many well-stocked bars I know of have had a variety of bottles gracing their shelves from the very beginning. Bitters are a distilled essence of a certain food, like celery or grapefruit. Adding a few drops of bitters to a cocktail or sparkling water can transform it, making an ordinary drink exceptional. Artisan makers are popping up in many regions, so good bitters are easier and easier to find.

# Balsamic Vinegar

**BALSAMIC VINEGAR HAS BEEN TRACED** as far back as 1046. Aged balsamic is a thing of real beauty, from both a visual and a flavor perspective. It's made from a reduction of pressed grapes, which are then aged for a minimum of twelve years in casks from different woods such as chestnut, acacia, and mulberry. The result is balsamic vinegar that is rich in both color and taste. Splurge on a bottle and use it in your next vinaigrette and you will be amazed. I think giving a bottle of balsamic vinegar instead of wine as a host or hostess gift is a creative alternative and will be enjoyed for much, much longer.

 **TED'S TIP**

Try wrapping up a bottle in a lovely white dish towel for a simple, stylish gift.

# Collections

CUSTOMERS AT MY SHOPS often ask me how to begin a collection. My first bit of advice to them is to begin collecting something they love or that brings them joy. It can be simple, or it can be grand, but most important, it should bring a smile to their faces when they look at it. We have a collection of Veuve champagne corks in an oversize glass bowl, which I have expanded over the years each time we enjoy a bottle. I walk by this simple collection each day, and it always brings me a bit of joy thinking about the many times we have enjoyed celebratory bottles. If you love walking on the beach, start a shell collection. These look beautiful stacked in a glass jar. If candlesticks are your thing, mass a grouping of them together to create an instant collection. Collect what you love, and you will rarely go wrong.

☞ TED'S TIP

Focus on the things you have, not on
the things you do not have. Be grateful
for what you have.

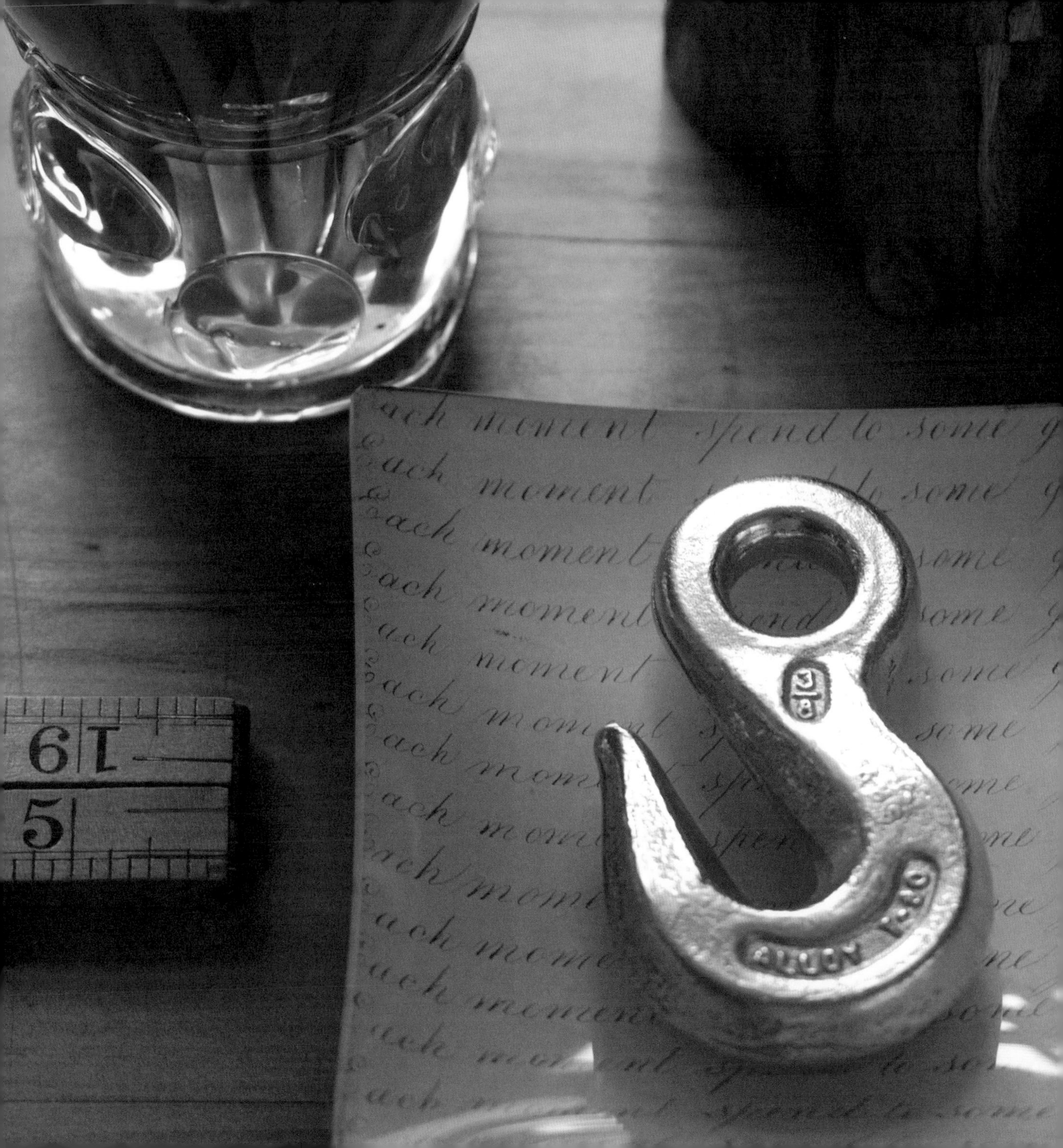

ach moment spend to some
6
5

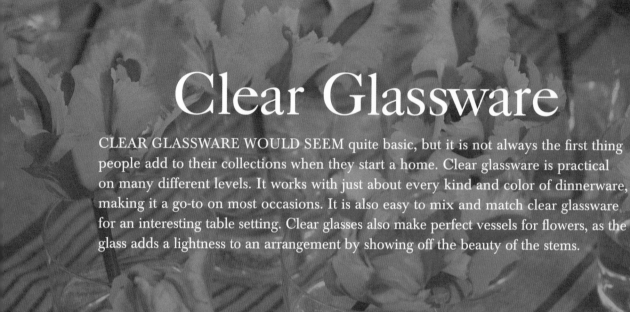

# Clear Glassware

CLEAR GLASSWARE WOULD SEEM quite basic, but it is not always the first thing people add to their collections when they start a home. Clear glassware is practical on many different levels. It works with just about every kind and color of dinnerware, making it a go-to on most occasions. It is also easy to mix and match clear glassware for an interesting table setting. Clear glasses also make perfect vessels for flowers, as the glass adds a lightness to an arrangement by showing off the beauty of the stems.

JUST HEARING THE WORD "CHAMPAGNE" conjures up happy thoughts. I wonder if the monk Dom Pérignon knew what a worldwide sensation he was creating when he took his first sip of champagne. There is something about that pop of a champagne cork that signals something good has, or is about, to happen—a proposal, promotion, birth, or marriage. However, the times I most enjoy a glass of champagne are when we are spending time with friends. An ordinary day can be transformed into extraordinary by just being together. Don't wait for a big event or for something momentous to enjoy a bottle; celebrate the small moments. Pour it in the finest glass you have and enjoy it as he did . . . "Come quickly, I am tasting the stars!"

Champagne

# Cuff Links

CUFF LINKS COMPLETELY SPIFF UP AN OUTFIT. They just do. A French-cuff shirt with a stylish pair of cuff links elevates the entire attire. Whether on a man or a woman, cuff links are an Old World accessory that are making a comeback. Well, in my world, they never really left. They make great gifts, especially for tough-to-buy-for guys. Men have so few options when it comes to adding a little personality to dressing, but the addition of cuff links bumps up the style quotient immensely. Cuff links that are personalized with initials make a very personal gift, as do versions with dates on them. Cuff links date back to the seventeenth century, when cuffs were tied together with ribbon; later, men began using small chains that were fastened to the end of a silver or gold button.

40

TED'S TIP

Look for cuff links on your travels. They are a lovely reminder of your trip each time you wear them.

# Candles

THE ACT OF LIGHTING A CANDLE can almost be a spiritual experience—the striking of the match, the lighting of the flame. Candles add so much to a home. They add drama to a dining table, scent to a bathroom, and a warm glow to a side table. Taper candles, pillar candles, scented candles in containers, votive candles—there is so much variety to choose from. I personally love unscented votives to scatter around a dining table, Glassybaby containers filled with tea lights to cast a glow around the house, and a Diptyque candle lit to throw off an amazing scent throughout our home. Really any combo will do. Just fill your space with candles and you will turn it into a magical domain once they all are lit. At the end of the day, I walk right in the door and light a candle as soon as we arrive home. There is something about the ritual that is immensely soothing. When we have guests, the task of lighting all the candles can take a bit of time. It almost becomes a form of meditation . . . the repetition of the match hitting the striker, the flame touching the wick and transferring the flame, creating light and warmth.

{ *Better to light a candle than to curse the darkness.* }
—Chinese Proverb

# Cherries

A BOWL OF WASHED CHERRIES sitting on the counter or in a gorgeous bowl on the dining table is a sight to be seen. The season for cherries can be short, but the taste and visual quotient can be quite high. Try setting out a small bowl of cherries next to a hunk of Spanish Manchego cheese at your next gathering. Try adding cherries and corn to an arugula salad for an exquisite flavor combination. Foods that are as pretty to look at as they are versatile to cook with excite me to no end, and the sweet cherry goes right to the top of that list.

# Cocktails

HAVING FRIENDS TO YOUR HOME for cocktails brings up thoughts of slower, more genteel times. It is a trend we are seeing more and more of, which I applaud loudly! A well-crafted cocktail can be a glorious sight, and I am not talking about a drink that requires twenty different ingredients. A simple gin and tonic can be perfection. Confidence and a few good ingredients are what make a great cocktail. Opening up your home is always a gracious act. Inviting a few friends or acquaintances over for cocktails is an easy way to entertain. I think some folks shy away from doing it, as they think they need a fully stocked bar—definitely not! Bottles of gin, vodka, and Scotch are great starters, as well as bottles of red and white wine. Choose flat-bottomed glassware that can easily stack. CB2 offers a glass called "Marta," which is ever so stylish and quite inexpensive, that we have used forever. Add a few mixers, a lemon, a lime, and a bag of ice, and you are good to go for a nice variety of cocktails. Open a jar of nuts, put out a good hunk of cheese with crackers, or fill a bowl with Goldfish crackers (Julia Child's favorite), and watch the cocktail party begin. Keep it simple—and remember to have a fun time at your own gathering.

## TED'S TIP

If you are hosting a large party, hire a bartender to make and serve drinks—trust me, it's a lifesaver. It also allows you to enjoy your own party.

*Roasting a chicken is one of those things that at first seems daunting, but once you get the hang of it I promise it will be something you will come back to time and again, and cook often. This is a one-pan recipe that is always a hit, whether for company or just a comforting evening at home.*

## ROAST CHICKEN

1 Preheat the oven to 400 degrees.
2 Rinse a 4- to 5-pound chicken and pat it dry with a paper towel.
3 Salt and pepper both the inside and outside of the bird.
4 Cut 1 clove of garlic in half and insert into the chicken's cavity with a sprig of rosemary.
5 Chop several onions; quarter your favorite type of potatoes; peel several medium-size carrots; break apart a few sprigs of rosemary. Place all in a roasting pan and mix together with olive oil.
6 Set the chicken on top of the onions, potatoes, carrots, and rosemary, as they will create a nice base for your bird.
7 Liberally rub the chicken with olive oil; salt and pepper all the contents of the pan, including the chicken again. (You really want the chicken well seasoned, so I like to do it before and after I slather it with the olive oil.)
8 Roast the chicken and vegetables in the oven for 1 hour and 15 minutes, occasionally mixing things around so the bottom layer does not burn.
9 Test the chicken with a meat thermometer; its temperature needs to be 165 degrees. If it is not quite there, roast a bit longer.
10 Take the chicken out of the pan once the meat has reached 165 degrees. Place on a plate, cover with aluminum foil, and let rest for 10 minutes.
11 Turn off the oven, but keep the pan of vegetables inside—so they stay nice and warm. Once the chicken has rested, you are all set to have a seriously scrumptious meal.

Chicken

# Dominoes

DOMINOES ARE BELIEVED TO HAVE ORIGINATED in China in the twelfth century and became very popular in Italy during the early eighteenth century. I am not so much drawn to dominoes for the gaming aspect, but rather for how beautifully each domino is constructed and what it is made out of. We always have bowls set around the shops with vintage dominoes placed in them. People buy them for a host of reasons, but generally a specific numeral resonates with them. The late author Nora Ephron was one of my customers and a fan of our vintage dominoes. I still think of her each time someone walks up to the register with a handful of dominoes. Whether made of bone or ivory inlaid over a dark wood such as ebony, vintage dominoes are little works of art.

# Drinks Table

HAVING A WELL-STOCKED BAR not only means having the right alcohol, but also having the right stuff to serve with it. Have things set out on a designated "drinks" table. I like to make a first drink for my guests, and by having all the ingredients out, they can later refill their own drinks. A nice bar setup will allow for many variations of drinks to be made. All of the below beverages work great as-is, too, so if you have a guest that would like a nonalcoholic drink or there are kids visiting, you are all set. Here is what we always try to have on hand:

- Club soda
- Tonic water
- Ginger ale and/or 7Up
- San Pellegrino grapefruit and blood orange soda
- V8 juice
- Perrier water

## ☞ TED'S TIP

Little treats, such as salted caramels given in cello bags as guests depart, end the evening on a sweet note. They are also tasty for the car or taxi ride home.

# Dish Towels

A GOOD DISH TOWEL IS SUCH A SIMPLE LUXURY. Even if you use your dishwasher for most dishes, you still occasionally have to wash and dry something fragile or non-dishwasher friendly. This is where a good dish towel comes into play. A beautiful cotton or linen dish towel feels good to the touch. It also does a great job of drying things, looking smart sitting out on the counter, or hanging up. My favorites are Le Jacquard Français towels from France, as well as vintage ones we pick up on our travels. We have had many of our French dish towels for years, as they keep getting better with age. I am also a big fan of using dish towels as oversize napkins. When you are serving a meal outside or serving a potentially messy meal, a dish towel becomes the perfect napkin.

☞ TED'S TIP

Use a cotton or linen napkin at each meal—it really elevates the experience of the meal, even if it's simple takeout.

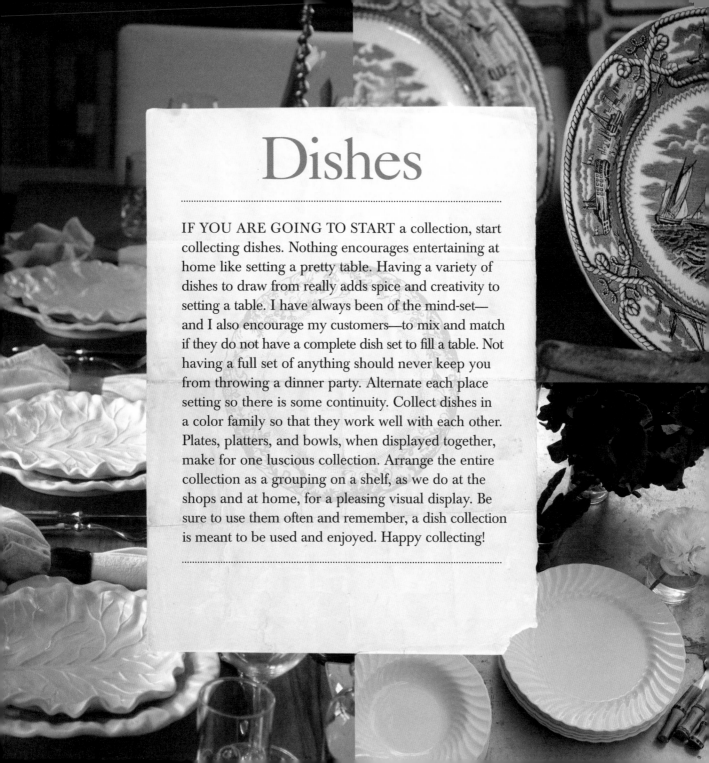

# Dishes

IF YOU ARE GOING TO START a collection, start collecting dishes. Nothing encourages entertaining at home like setting a pretty table. Having a variety of dishes to draw from really adds spice and creativity to setting a table. I have always been of the mind-set—and I also encourage my customers—to mix and match if they do not have a complete dish set to fill a table. Not having a full set of anything should never keep you from throwing a dinner party. Alternate each place setting so there is some continuity. Collect dishes in a color family so that they work well with each other. Plates, platters, and bowls, when displayed together, make for one luscious collection. Arrange the entire collection as a grouping on a shelf, as we do at the shops and at home, for a pleasing visual display. Be sure to use them often and remember, a dish collection is meant to be used and enjoyed. Happy collecting!

DAHLIAS ARE SUCH INCREDIBLE FLOWERS. They are works of art, really. Blooming in the late summer through the middle of autumn, dahlias provide a great variety of display options. They look spectacular in single-stem vases, since each bloom is so singularly beautiful. The size alone sometimes makes this a necessity. They also work perfectly bunched tightly together in a vase, with the heads just reaching over the top. A stroll through Seattle's Pike Place Market stalls in the late summer, when a profusion of dahlias are for sale, is one of those mind-altering experiences—it is heaven, pure heaven.

50

{*I must have flowers, always, always.*}
—Claude Monet

# Ephemera

EPHEMERA IS DEFINED IN THE DICTIONARY as *paper items, such as menus or ticket stubs, that were originally meant to be discarded after use but have since become collected.* I think ephemera has a place in almost everyone's life. Ephemera is a great reminder of where you have been, of a certain meal you enjoyed, or of a great movie you saw. Ephemera, in some ways, is a biography of your life. The artist Picasso was an incredible collector of this material, which was amassed into a show we attended in Paris at Musée National Picasso some years ago. It was like reading a book of his life, but through snippets of paper tickets, letters, menus, and the like. I like to use ephemera to line the inside of my closet, or I might use a piece as a bookmark. You can simply collect things along the way and put them in a box. It will be such a treat to open it at a later time and be reminded of your journey through life.

{ *Treasure this day and treasure yourself.*
*Truly, neither will ever happen again.*
—*Ray Bradbury* }

## TED'S TIP

Give away tickets. We have friends with season tickets to just about everything. Every once in a while, we get a call offering tickets to something they cannot attend. It's an out-of-the-blue treat to see a performance at the last minute.

3

Mr. Ted Kennedy Watson

Watson Kennedy Fine Living
86 Pine St.
Seattle, WA.

98101

ERNEST HEMINGWAY
1899 - 1999

BAR HEMINGWAY

Ritz Paris

HOTEL
LE TOURVILLE

Paris

TICKET

# Eyewear

COOL EYEWEAR used to be something that required a second mortgage—not any longer. With online resources such as Warby Parker as well as a slew of other smaller companies cropping up, spiffy frames are now more readily available than ever. Eyeglasses make interesting little vignettes, too. Set a couple of pairs out in a row on a dresser and allow them to become a rotating art piece, where form meets function.

# Edison Bulbs

EDISON BULBS HAVE BEEN MAKING A
CREATIVE COMEBACK in the last few years.
The glow they release is magical. The filament
threads make the bulbs into little works of art. I
like to use them in sconces and vintage alabaster
lamps and leave them exposed, without a shade.
The look is Old World with a fresh twist, and is
fun in both modern and vintage interiors.

# Eggs

OH, THE SIMPLICITY OF EGGS. You can buy good-quality and quite beautiful eggs at your local grocery store. I used to have to go to a farmers' market or a farm stand to get such high-quality eggs. While those are still great options, a good egg is now available to all, to use in recipes, to whip up for breakfast, or to just admire in a bowl on the counter. Be on the lookout for an interesting egg holder for your refrigerator to display your eggs in. We use a simple white dish and each time I open the door and see the eggs, it makes me happy. Ahhhh, the beauty of an egg is timeless.

# Flash Cards

VINTAGE FLASH CARDS HAVE BEEN a staple at Watson Kennedy for many years. We have baskets and baskets of them. Educational flash cards are great for art projects, framing, and bookmarks. The heavy card stock and patina of years of usage make them a wonderful collectible item. They also make for truly memorable cards for any occasion.

AS YOU PROBABLY HAVE ALREADY NOTICED from this book or from reading my blog or looking at my shop website, I am crazy for flowers. Flowers add so much to a life, to a room, and to the soul. Flowers add life, color, and visual interest. Whether plucked from your own garden, purchased at the corner grocery store, or expertly arranged by a florist, flowers need not always be thought of as an extravagance. Arrange them simply or arrange them like a Dutch master painting, but include them often in your daily life and they will just make you happy—very happy.

## TED'S TIP

Keep flowers cut low on the dining table so guests can see one another and can converse easily.

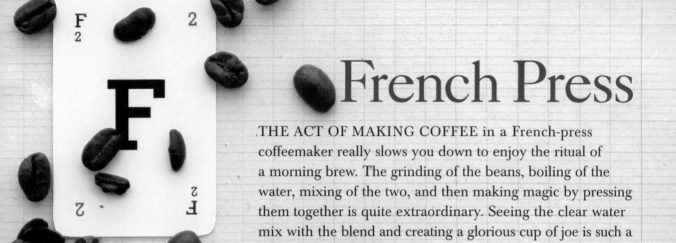

# French Press

THE ACT OF MAKING COFFEE in a French-press coffeemaker really slows you down to enjoy the ritual of a morning brew. The grinding of the beans, boiling of the water, mixing of the two, and then making magic by pressing them together is quite extraordinary. Seeing the clear water mix with the blend and creating a glorious cup of joe is such a sight. Plus, the beauty of a French press sitting on a breakfast table elevates the specialness of the meal, and of the ritual.

{ *There are people whom one loves and appreciates immediately and forever. Even to know they are alive in this world is quite enough.* }

—Nancy Spain

# Frittata

*Sunday mornings are a pretty relaxing time at the Watson–Sive household. It usually means eggs of some sort, since the eggs we buy at the farm stands on Vashon Island are pretty amazing. A frittata is another one of my go-to egg dishes to make, as you can really mix it up by using lots of different ingredients to make a myriad of variations, such as mushrooms with parmesan or caramelized shallots with chèvre. The following smoked salmon with herbed chèvre version has become a new favorite and works perfectly cut in half to serve two.*

## SMOKED SALMON AND CHÈVRE FRITTATA

1. Break 5 eggs into a bowl.
2. Add a splash of milk, a few pinches of salt, and a pinch of pepper, and whisk together.
3. Turn on the broiler in your oven to heat up.
4. Using a nonstick skillet that can go into the oven, turn the stove burner to the lowest setting and add enough butter so the skillet is fully coated once the butter melts.
5. Add the egg mixture to the skillet.
6. Add crumbled bits of smoked salmon and scatter bits of herbed goat cheese around the eggs.
7. Let the eggs cook just until they have set on the bottom, but are still runny on top.
8. Take the skillet and place under the broiler (you want to stay with this dish as it cooks). The eggs will start to bubble, brown, and puff up.
9. Once the entire mixture is set, take it out from under the broiler, making sure to wear a heat-proof cooking glove, pot holder, or oven mitt, as the handle will be quite hot.
10. Serve with toast. This dish also makes a lovely lunch or summer supper served with a salad and a glass of Chardonnay.

# Flea Markets

A GOOD FLEA MARKET is a sight to behold. There is something about so many objects amassed into one area that makes my heart skip a beat. Most objects that are bought at flea markets have great soul, and will be cherished things in your home. You just have to prepare yourself to see quite a bit of bad stuff . . . but then, ahhhh, you spot a diamond in the rough! Behold, the beauty of a flea market. Do a Google search and see which ones are near you. While my favorites are in Paris and London—well, probably the fact that they *are* in Paris and London might have something to do with that!—there are many good ones that take place in the United States as well. These are some favorites:

- Porte de Vanves and Porte de Clignancourt, both in Paris
- Portobello Road in London
- Alameda Point Antiques Faire in California
- Brimfield Antique Show and Flea Market in Massachusetts
- Brooklyn Flea in New York
- Rose Bowl Flea Market in Pasedena, California
- Daytona Flea & Farmers Market in Florida

☞ TED'S TIP

Donate an article of clothing you have not worn in over a year. Just think of the comfort it will bring to someone in need.

*I chose feta for my list because it is a cheese with a fairly long shelf life, which makes it easy to have a block of it on hand in your fridge when you need it. Feta usually comes from Greece, but you can also find great feta from France and from the United States. It is a brined curd cheese that comes typically in block form. I find it is best to buy it this way as opposed to crumbled, as it lasts much longer—plus, it's fun to crumble it yourself. Easily added to salads and pasta dishes, feta is something you will find yourself reaching for time and again when whipping up creative meals. One of my favorite go-to easy recipes is a super lemony orzo with feta. It's easy to assemble. Be sure to use fresh lemon juice, since it's one of the major ingredients, and your best extra virgin olive oil.*

## LEMON ORZO WITH FETA

1 Combine the zest of 2 lemons with 1 cup freshly squeezed lemon juice and 1 cup olive oil.

2 Add a generous amount of salt and pepper.

3 Whisk everything together and set aside.

4 Boil a large pot of salted water.

5 Add 16 ounces of orzo pasta and cook until it is al dente.

6 Once the pasta is done, drain and immediately place into a large bowl.

7 While the pasta is still hot, add the lemon and olive oil vinaigrette. With a fork, fluff until all of the liquid is incorporated into the pasta.

8 Let the pasta sit to cool so that it absorbs all of that lemony goodness. Finally, add some big chunks of feta and enjoy!

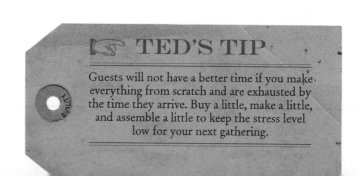

## ☞ TED'S TIP

Guests will not have a better time if you make everything from scratch and are exhausted by the time they arrive. Buy a little, make a little, and assemble a little to keep the stress level low for your next gathering.

Feta

RONZ

Orzo

# Farmers' Markets & Farm Stands

BUYING PRODUCE AND FLOWERS from a farmers' market or a farm stand is a good thing. Not only are you supporting a local farmer, which means supporting a local business, but you are also buying produce that is grown with tremendous care and love. Plus, you are buying food that is almost always really good for you. It might cost a bit more money, but the end result is so very worth it. It is also a visual feast, so you are treated to a lively show in the process. We like to arrange all we have purchased into a little tableau on a platter in the kitchen right as we unpack it—a sort of real-life "still life" painting. There are more and more farmers' markets popping up each year, so check your local paper to see if there's one in your area.

68

## TED'S TIP

Keep fresh flowers at home and, if you can swing it, a flower on your desk at work.

G

A SYMBOL FOR GROWTH, the color green looks great in any shade. It works beautifully to brighten a room while also rooting the space. Green pottery, green linens, green lamp shades—all create such a positive energy and vibe for a space. We always have an all-green display going at the shops. These are the first areas that customers gravitate to. We have an all-green kitchen filled with varying shades of the hue. Toaster, food processor, bowls, glassware, flatware, plates, they all make the space a happy, vibrant place to cook and to be. Some of my favorite green paints are:

Pratt & Lambert: Moss Green 16-29

Farrow & Ball: Folly Green 76

Farrow & Ball: Cooking Apple Green 32

Sherwin-Williams: Leapfrog 6431

Benjamin Moore: Chic Lime 396

Benjamin Moore: Potpourri Green 2029-50

# Green

FILLED GLASS CONTAINERS can add a spot of color to a kitchen, desktop, or laundry room. Clear glass containers are what I am most drawn to, as they really allow the objects that are placed in them to truly shine. Think simple, glass, airtight jars filled with cooking supplies (sugar, nuts, flour, or cereal) lined up on shelving. Not only do you get the enjoyment of seeing what is in the jars, but it makes it easy to see what you need when you are creating a list for your next grocery shopping trip. On a desktop, glass containers can hold paper clips, pens, extra staples—all ready at your fingertips so you are not fumbling through drawers looking for supplies. Simple glass containers are also perfect vessels for holding bunches of flowers you can pick up at the corner market.

Glass Containers

# G&Ts

AHHHH, THE APPEAL OF A GIN AND TONIC is timeless, summer in a glass—or really anytime you want to re-create summer. There are so many cocktail options out there, but a G&T is just one of the classics that folks come back to time and time again. Use a good gin (Hendrick's and Tanqueray are personal favorites) and a good tonic; add ice cubes; squeeze the juice of a lime wedge into the glass; add the wedge; and *voilà!*—a gin and tonic. I like to make a big grouping on a large vintage silver platter, creating an instant party feel. So often, the simplest things are the best.

☞ TED'S TIP

Relax and have a good time at your own dinner or party.

An important phase of crop production is the selection of seed. Crop seeds of different kinds have certain definite characters that are used as aids in identification and the determination of their quality. Weed seeds ... farmer ... seeds bought and planted by the farmer ... of his life to control or eradicate them. It is highly important that everyone with the responsibility of seed selection should know what to look for.

OBJECT: To become acquainted with the appearance of common crop and weed seeds.

DIRECTIONS:

# Geraniums

74

**GERANIUM PLANTS ARE INCREDIBLY HEARTY.** They are easy to care for and, when placed in a light-filled space, they will grow like weeds—*good* weeds. My favorite usage for these gorgeous flowers is to cut the stems when they start to get leggy and use the cuttings in single-stem vases. They add a bit of life to a room. My friend Catherine, who is a floral maestro, introduced me to the scented variety years ago, and I have never looked back. If you have the choice, always opt for the scented variety. My favorites are the mint-scented rose geranium, the Prince Rupert, and the peppermint geranium. The leaves of these varieties tend to have more variation, and they release a beautiful scent when you rub your fingers on them. They are also lovely just left in a pretty container on a dining or side table.

c. Note luster.

d. Immature seeds are usually lighter in color. Use darkest color as characteristic one. Old seeds are ...

{ *We are cups, constantly and quietly being filled.*
*The trick is knowing how to tip ourselves*
*over and let the beautiful out.* }
—*Ray Bradbury*

3. After studying mount permanently from the pans for reference.

4. Learn common name. Scientific name will be of value and should also be put on seed mount with common name.

# Hyacinths

HYACINTHS ARE ONE OF THE KINDS OF FLOWERS that signal spring is well underway and that summer is right around the corner. In addition to being such a pretty cluster of flowers, they are also quite fragrant. Cultivated commercially since the sixteenth century, hyacinths became very popular in eighteenth- and early nineteenth-century Europe. In the Victorian language of flowers, the hyacinth symbolizes sport or play. I prefer them in a single bunch without any other type of flower in the container—just a large mass of extraordinary hyacinths. If you change the water regularly, you will be rewarded with a very long life for your flowers and will see each stem's tiny blossoms open all the way, releasing a heady scent into the air.

# Hydrangeas

HYDRANGEAS ARE SUCH HAPPY PLANTS and come in myriad shapes, sizes, and colors. They are a mix of hearty and delicate, which makes having them in your life so pleasant. If you have a place to plant them in your yard, certainly do. They work beautifully grown in pots, which look nice on a deck. If you do not have an outdoor space, a hydrangea plant slipped into a decorative container will add great color and energy to any home. The blooms look stellar in vases, either solo or mixed with a flower like a rose. Hydrangeas are also quite lovely dried and then massed together for a perpetual arrangement. However you see fit, having hydrangeas in your life will bring you much happiness.

NOTHING MAKES ME HAPPIER at our mailbox than finding a handwritten note tucked in the mounds of everyday mail. I'm always touched by the thought, time, and care shown by the sender. I am a firm believer in the handwritten note. What stops most people from sending notes is lack of preparation. To help make writing quick thank-you notes—and notes in general—easier, have a box or drawer with all of the supplies needed to make it happen quickly and efficiently. I am a big fan of Dempsey & Carroll from New York. They create a lovely variety of note cards that have a beautiful singular image and are blank, so you can use them for any occasion. Having stationery at the ready really makes the task of letter and note writing a joy, instead of an arduous task. Here are some helpful ideas:

1 Keep a nice variety of cards that you pick up randomly as you shop. The best value is always boxed cards, and buying in volume applies to cards as well. I tend to buy cards that are "un-greeted," meaning they are blank on the inside. I always feel you can express a sentiment for a friend better than with something generic written for you.

2 Each time you are at the post office, check to see what stock they have of cool-looking stamps. If they strike your fancy, buy them and start a collection. Nothing hinders note and letter writing more than lack of stamps.

3 Be sure to use a pen you enjoy writing with. What is your style? Maybe you like writing with blue ink. Maybe you like trying calligraphy when you write a note. Have a variety of writing instruments alongside your cards and stamps.

4 Maintain easy access to addresses. Whether you keep an address book or a file on your computer, an organized list is essential to getting notes out quickly.

5 Create a spot in your home where you feel comfortable writing. You don't always have to write at a desk. My favorite spot to write notes is at our dining table, which allows me to spread all of my supplies out.

6 Most important, remember that you do not need to write a novel—or even a novella. A few quick lines written on beautiful stationery and sent with a cool stamp will be such a welcome treat for any recipient.

# Handwritten Notes

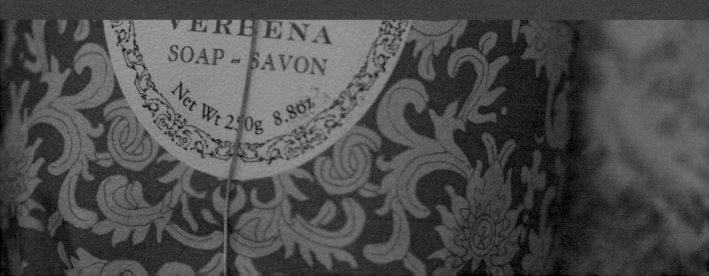

# Hand Soap

ANY ITEM THAT IS PART OF A DAILY ROUTINE can elevate it to "nicer" routine by bumping up the quality quotient, and hand soap does just that. A beautiful bar of French-milled soap makes washing or bathing such a glorious experience. Washing your hands with a great liquid soap in the bathroom or at the kitchen sink makes the entire act so much more pleasurable. I am a big fan of Molton Brown liquid hand soap from England as well as Fresh bar soap from France. Both have been Watson Kennedy staples for years. Whatever brand you like, just keep a few extra bars or bottles on hand so you never run out.

# Herbs

ROSEMARY, DILL, THYME, MINT, OREGANO, BASIL, CHIVES, AND PARSLEY are just some of the many herbs that can be used in a variety of ways. Using fresh herbs is a must, since they elevate the experience of cooking, but herbs also work beautifully all by themselves in a pinch as a solo arrangement. They are also lovely when mixed into a bouquet with flowers. I love mixing sprigs of rosemary with zinnias in late summer for a spirited arrangement. Use mint for its lovely shade of green, and mix with pink roses or pink peonies. If nothing excites you at the flower market or grocery store, try putting an assortment of fresh herbs in simple drinking glasses at each guest's place setting for a quick and easy appealing hit of green at your next dinner. Growing herbs is a pretty easy thing—and I have no green thumb. Try a few pots on a windowsill, or venture outside and try growing them in a large pot or a patch of earth. Trust me, you will be happy you tried, and greatly rewarded for your efforts. If you look after your herbs with frequent watering, they will grow like weeds.

# Hammered Aluminum

HAMMERED ALUMINUM SAW ITS START in the 1920s, but really took off and became incredibly popular in the 1930s when the pieces were often given as wedding gifts. We began our collection when we received a hammered aluminum ice bucket as a wedding gift—it passed down to us. I've added this beautiful item to my list because it is an affordable vintage piece that makes for great gift giving or a collection. Antique malls and flea markets tend to have a profusion of it, which always helps to keep the prices down. You can still find gorgeous platters, trays, bowls, and, my particular favorite, ice buckets. The material is lightweight, with many pieces having an embossed image.

WHETHER MADE INTO CUPS, necklaces, spoons, or spreaders, horn is a natural material that has so much glorious variation that each piece always ends up being one of a kind. Most horn today comes from ram, buffalo, or cows, as the raw material is exclusively a by-product of the meat industry and of natural death. When heated, horn becomes pliable and can then be formed and cut to make goods. A product made of horn adds character and interest. I am especially fond of horn cups to hold pencils on a desk and horn-handled knives to use when serving cheese.

# Horn

# Hotel Silver

THE THING I MOST LIKE ABOUT HOTEL SILVER is that it is meant to be used and enjoyed. Many silver pieces are purely decorative and not food-safe. Hotel silver was used by hotel guests from the turn of the last century through the 1960s and held myriad items, such as teapots, coffeepots, toast holders, compotes, bowls, and trays. Popular in Europe and the United States, hotel silver can still be found at antique malls and flea markets, as well as retailers such as Watson Kennedy and Bergdorf Goodman. Given the desirability, prices can be steep—but so very worth it, as you will get many years of enjoyment out of each piece. Many of the pieces are stamped with the hotel name, which increases their appeal. Hotel silver has a history to each piece—just think of the stories it could tell.

## ☞ TED'S TIP

The easiest way to start a hotel silver collection is begin with one type of item, like knives, and add to that first. Put them into a clear glass standing upright and leave them out on your counter to use often and enjoy each time you look at them.

# Honey

HONEY OVER THE YEARS HAS ATTRACTED many artisan beekeepers, who bottle limited amounts of sublime honey. Added to tea, spread on toast, or included in a recipe, honey is a sweet addition to anything it touches. Keep an assortment at the ready. A bottle of honey makes a usable gift, so pick some up on your travels. I like to give a bottle of honey instead of a bottle of wine as a host or hostess gift. Honey is a fabulous addition to a cheese platter at a cocktail or dinner party.

{ *We are all travelers in the wilderness of this world, and the best we can find in our travels is an honest friend.* }
—*Robert Lewis Stevenson*

# Ice Cubes

OF COURSE, THE FIRST THOUGHT is that an ice "cube" would be square, but that is so rarely the case. Ice most often is served crushed, half mooned, or round—all of which melt rather quickly. Extra-large ice cube trays have started showing up more and more on kitchen shop shelves, which makes finding them quite easy. The extra-large size allows for a slower melting of the ice, thus watering your drink down less. Plus, the cube just looks fun in your glass. I spent an early part of an evening waiting for an old college friend who was meeting me for dinner in New York. I sat at the bar at Freemans enjoying a cocktail and was treated to a show from the bartender crushing square ice cubes into submission for crushed ice—dinner theater at its finest.

90

ICE BUCKETS HAD BECOME A THING OF THE PAST over the years, but they are starting to catch on again. And I say we should revive the tradition of having an ice bucket on the counter or snugly placed on a little bar. Whether crystal, silver, glass, hammered aluminum, or lacquer, an ice bucket not only does the supreme duty of holding ice, but it also looks so darn stylish while doing so. In a pinch, an ice bucket can make a wondrous vase when you are presented with a hearty bouquet at your next dinner party. I cannot begin to tell you how often I have used our ice buckets for this very purpose.

Always have an extra bag of ice at the ready. A full
ice bucket can be a thing of beauty!

# Italian Wrapping Paper

ITALIAN WRAPPING PAPER TAKES WRAPPING GIFTS to a whole new level. The Italians do paper so beautifully. Italian wrapping paper has a feel to it like very few others. When you fold down the corners, the paper creases perfectly. Now let's talk patterns: Italian paper comes in so many classic varieties, with Florentine being a personal favorite. The colors are saturated and vibrant, which makes them not only great for gift-wrapping, but also fantastic for art projects. When you see this paper, pick it up and feel it. You will notice a difference instantly. Good stuff.

# Jam Jars

USING EVERYDAY ITEMS that otherwise would be discarded after use is a fun way to start a collection. Having a large number of any one item can be visually appealing when massed together. Old jam jars provide great storage for everyday things that are also singularly visually appealing, such as peppercorns, dried apricots, and herbs. Jam jars also work swimmingly for make-ahead drinks for a picnic, as the lid seals the liquid tight inside the jar for travel. They are utilitarian items with great flair—if put to use once the jam has been enjoyed.

{ *Simplify, simplify, simplify! Simplicity of life and elevation of purpose.* }
—Henry David Thoreau

VINTAGE KNIVES ARE GREAT to look for on trips to flea markets and thrift stores. Bone, sterling silver, mother-of-pearl—there is such variety out there. They make for wonderful letter openers, and are also spectacular as cheese knives. A variety of them in a vintage glass makes for a stylish vignette. Like vintage keys, vintage knives have a history and a story to tell.

# Knives

# Keys

WELL, VINTAGE KEYS TO BE EXACT. We have seen a real influx of the usage of keys in design, particularly jewelry, in the last few years. I think the vintage key craze is here to stay. Skeleton keys are visually interesting design objects, and having them out on display is a smart thing. We always have a bowl filled with vintage keys for sale at my shops. It's always interesting to see which one a person will gravitate to. In fact, we have a regular customer who has bought hundreds over the years. She gives them away to friends and complete strangers as small gifts and tokens. Trust me. Try holding a skeleton key in your hand; you will feel something.

*A bowl full of lemons is a sight to behold. Whether a slice in a glass of sparkling water, a few cut up with roast chicken, or as a basic ingredient for a quick and easy vinaigrette, lemons never disappoint. When the world hands you lemons, I say make this delightfully tasty vinaigrette. Since it has so few ingredients, the fresh lemon juice and some really good olive oil are key. I love to make extra of this vinaigrette and put it into little Weck jars to give as simple gifts. When Meyer lemons are in season, I will juice a bagful and keep the freshly squeezed lemon juice in the fridge at the ready. All winter long, we get to enjoy the fruits—well, actually the liquids—of my labor. It is perfect for when a recipe calls for a little fresh lemon juice.*

## LEMON VINAIGRETTE

1 Squeeze 1 fresh lemon to obtain 2 tablespoons of fresh lemon juice.
2 In a bowl, add 1 teaspoon of Dijon mustard to the lemon juice.
3 Add a few healthy pinches of salt and a pinch of pepper.
4 Whisk in a ¼ cup of the best extra virgin olive oil you have.

# Lemons

☞ TED'S TIP

Add a fresh lemon slice
to your daily water.

# Locker Baskets

BY NOW, DEAR READER, you have probably clued into the fact that I like old things. More so, that I really love them. I find they have such a special place in our lives. Using something vintage, old, or antique is one of the best forms of recycling. If we have to live with "stuff" in our lives, it might as well be really great stuff. And that is where vintage locker baskets come into play. You can find these at antique malls, flea markets, and shops such as mine. Use them for holding things, or attach them to a wall and have them hold more things. They have a great industrial aesthetic, are hugely practical, and have a utilitarian vibe to them.

# Lucite

LUCITE IS ONE OF THOSE MATERIALS that works in both modern and vintage interiors. Lucite adds a freshness to any room that has it. Perhaps you have a Lucite tray to hold the contents of a small bar on a side table, or a Lucite console behind a sofa to add room for a lamp and other objects. Regardless of its use, Lucite is always a winning design option and quite stylish. The material was developed in 1928, and later brought to market by the Rohm and Haas Company under the trademark of Plexiglas.

# Letters

WE SELL BOWL AFTER BOWL full of letters in a variety of fonts that folks buy for a host of reasons: to embellish an envelope while adding the recipient's initials, to spell out a favorite word, or to add to a creative art project. Whatever the task, letters personalize a space as well as a gift. Vintage game-piece letters work perfectly in place of name cards to let your guests know where you would like them to sit at your next dinner party. Oversize letters become a work of art when hung or propped up in a bookcase, signifying the inhabitants' initials.

{ *A thing of beauty is a joy forever.* }
—*John Keats*

MONOGRAMMING PERSONALIZES THINGS in a special way. A bag given with the recipient's initials or house name (see **Naming Your Home**) shows the giver went the extra mile to make the gift extra special. A shirt with a monogram on the pocket brands it to the owner. It is a personal way to make an item truly yours. For me personally, it's the monogrammed L.L.Bean bag. I have carried one of these bags around with me since I was young and traveled to tennis tournaments. They are hands down the most durable and best value for a bag out there. I thoroughly love this bag, and it's one of our favorite gifts to give when someone has a baby, buys a new home, or just deserved a personalized gift. A monogrammed boat-and-tote bag also makes a great receptacle for carrying a variety of gifts when you need a holder for all the goodies. They come in a host of handle colors and monogram thread colors.

# Monogramming

# Multiples of Things

THINK STRENGTH IN NUMBERS on this one. A few bowls hung up in a row is pretty, but quite a few bowls hung up in a row is even prettier. Multiples of one type of object are such a strong visual. Think of a fireplace mantel covered with candlesticks. When you use a good number of the same object, the eye looks at the collective whole as one, and you can create a really stunning display of items. Think also of a dining table filled with clear drinking glasses, each glass filled with a tulip. From the simple to the grand, mass a collection together for awesome visual impact.

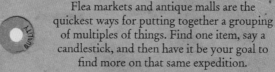

☞ TED'S TIP

Flea markets and antique malls are the quickest ways for putting together a grouping of multiples of things. Find one item, say a candlestick, and then have it be your goal to find more on that same expedition.

*Whether you make it with gin or vodka (we are gin folk), knowing how to make a martini is one of those simple things many shy away from. So when you do make them, you really do shine. Below is my recipe. I find the colder the gin is, the better—it is best when the bottle has just come out of the freezer. It is pretty darn simple, yet pretty darn fabulous.*

1  Pour 3 to 4 ounces, depending on the glass size, into a shaker filled with ice.
2  Add ½ to 1 ounce vermouth. I prefer just a tad; others prefer more.
3  Put the lid on and shake, shake, shake.
4  Pour into a martini glass that has 2 skewered olives in it.

Martini

# Music {Sheet}

VINTAGE SHEET MUSIC is something I started using in displays at my shops from the very beginning. I also used it in my wholesale showroom. There is something about the weight of the paper and the yellowing of the sheets that is so appealing. The pages with the music notes make for great art projects or can be tucked under a plate for a makeshift place mat in a pinch. These can be collected at tag sales and flea markets. I look at using the old sheets as recycling at its finest. To be able to enjoy the beauty of the pages—instead of having them just sit in a drawer, falling out of a music book— brings them back to life. Even if you cannot read music—I certainly do not—the rhythmic patterns are visually appealing. We also run old music sheets through our paper shredder to make filler for gift boxes.

# Naming Your Home

WHY NOT? This practice should not be reserved for old, stately English manor homes. Whether you live in a studio apartment or a grand mansion, naming your home makes it more personal. "Come for drinks at seven to the Gainsborough" sounds much more intimate than just giving your street address. It adds a specialness to your home. We often give a gift of a personalized item (notepads or a tote bag) with the house name on it when we are weekend guests.

OVER THE YEARS, friends have given me abandoned bird nests that they find. I like to put the nest under a cloche to protect it and add a bit of importance. My love of all things bird runs deep, and nests have ended up being some of my very favorite possessions. They bring the outdoors in, and they serve as a constant reminder to slow down and enjoy the task at hand. Watching a bird make a nest is a pretty magical experience. Bit by bit, item by item, they build a nest that is a small work of art. I like to think of a home as a nest and, bit by bit, over time, we make it just how we want it.

{ *Thoughts, rest your wings. Here is a hollow of silence, a nest of stillness, in which to hatch your dreams.* }
*—Joan Walsh Anglund*

# Nests

# Outdoor Shower

LET'S BE CLEAR on this one: When I say an outdoor shower, I mean one with copious amounts of hot water. I have seen outdoor shower kits where one hooks it up to a garden hose, and *voilà!*—an outdoor shower. This is not what I have in mind. There truly are few things that beat showering outside under the sun, or the stars, which turns an ordinary shower into a magical experience. My first experiences with an outdoor shower were at a lovely manse in Northeast Harbor, Maine, and then later at the cabin of our dear friend Cara Wells in Southold, on Long Island's North Fork. This prompted us to work an outdoor shower into our plan out at WestWard, our beach home on Vashon Island.

We had a simple wood platform built to house the shower, and then loaded it with pots of scented geraniums to add color and scent while we shower. If it works to install an outdoor shower next to your home, preferably with loads of privacy and a view—of your garden, of the mountains, of the water—then by all means grab the opportunity. You will be so happy you did. Heaven, pure heaven, I tell you.

DINING OUTDOORS CAN OFTENTIMES BE HEAVENLY. If getting an additional table is not in the cards—and if the scenario works—take your dining table outside and have your meal. This is what we do at our Vashon Island home. Breakfast, lunch, dinner—all are immediately improved when you dine out in the open air. Set the table with your finest linens and flatware for a memorable meal. Candles, flowers, ephemera—all should be added. That extra bit of effort will be well worth it!

Honor the meal.

# Outdoor Dining

# Oysters

NOT ONLY ARE OYSTERS WONDERFUL to dine on, but you can use the shells for projects after they have been enjoyed. My favorite thing to do with oyster shells is to make a bed of them in a glass container, place paperwhite narcissus bulbs on top, and then put down another layer of oyster shells. Once the bulbs start to grow, it is beautiful to see bits of the shells poking out from the shoots. They also work well running down a window ledge as a reminder of the beach and sea. The varying shades of white and gray are so soothing. Before you use the shells in a project, place them in a pot of boiling water and boil away. Repeat if necessary. Then, wash the shells with soap and water.

# Orchid

AN ORCHID IS ONE OF THOSE FLOWERS
and plants that conjures up thoughts of the good life.
This exotic flower adds beauty to any space it graces.
Over the years, the price of more readily available
orchids has come down considerably, and they
are now quite affordable. Orchids can last for an
amazingly long time if cared for properly. We have
had friends who cared for the same orchid plants
for years. Recently, our local grocer had a table
full of orchid plants for ten dollars a pot. Vintage
champagne buckets are my favorite choice to house
an orchid. I place old champagne corks on top of the
dirt, creating a whimsical home for the plant.

*Find the seed at the bottom of your*
*heart and bring forth a flower.*
—Shigenori Kameoka

# Olive Oil

EXTRA VIRGIN OLIVE OIL, TO BE EXACT, will change how you think and use olive oil. I did not think there was much of a difference, but there really is. A good extra virgin olive oil can transform a plain vinaigrette into something sublime. I am a big fan of Grove 45 or B.R. Cohn, both of which are from Northern California, but I love a good Italian or French variety, too. Aside from tasting great, extra virgin olive oil is also a healthy alternative to butter. Roasting vegetables bathed in extra virgin olive oil on a sheet pan in a hot oven will ensure you eat every veggie on your plate. In addition, a bottle of olive oil is one of our go-to gifts in place of a bottle of wine when we go to a dinner party. Both are roughly the same price, and the enjoyment of a nice olive oil will be long remembered.

PLATES ARE ONE OF THOSE THINGS that are easy to form into a collection. They are practical to stack, so they do not take up much room. A mix-and-match table with a variety of plates can be quite stylish. Plates also look great hung on a wall, so they can become artwork of a sort. Antique stores, flea markets, and kitchen shops are all great places to hunt for plates. I encourage customers to start with white plates to begin a collection, and expand to color plates once the collection is well underway. White plates are like white pottery; they work with almost anything. They also make food look quite fetching sitting atop them. Mix old with new for a fresh look that you can call your own.

## TED'S TIP

Use your nice china. I repeat, use it, use it, use it. This stuff is not to be saved for a special day. If it breaks, know that it was well used and well loved.

# Plates

A LIFE WELL LIVED really is all about seeing and relishing all the small details that fill our days. I find focusing in on even the smallest of details really bumps up the enjoyment quotient of an experience and a space. An example would be pushpins. There are some very stylish pushpins out there, so taking a little extra time to find ones that resonate with you can change how you use them. The late, great Albert Hadley used red-headed pushpins on his inspiration boards, which suited him to a T, as he was such a fan of the color red. I love pushpins with numbers on them. I get inspired seeing them scattered all along the corkboard in my office—details, details, details.

# Pushpins

A CONTAINER FILLED WITH PAPERWHITE NARCISSUS BULBS MAKES ME HAPPY. It is a signal that the holidays are rapidly approaching for most folks, and if you are a retailer like me, that means crunch time. The papery white petals and intoxicating aroma fill the shops and our home, also adding that bit of green I long for in the beginning of the cooler winter months. Not only are they pretty and great smelling, they are also one hearty little bulb and incredibly easy to grow. Start by finding your favorite glass vessels. My favorite is a large, rather thick jar that sits on our kitchen counter and has a festive green lid. Line the bottom of the jar with champagne corks, rocks, or whatever pleases you, as long as it can take being submerged in water. This will help to elevate the bulbs so they are not sitting too deep in the water. I find it best to really crowd the bulbs and have them butting right up to one another; once they start to grow, this helps keep them from falling over. I then put a few extra champagne corks in any open spots as I like to see a bit of the cork once the bulbs start their magic. Then, add just enough water so the bottom of the bulb is touching the water. You will be amazed at how quickly these take root. It's as easy as that. Just make sure the water level remains where it started. I find having them in a tall-necked container is helpful, as once the stems lengthen, they are held upright by the jar and do not fall over—a common complaint I hear about these lovelies. Enjoy!

# Paperwhite Narcissus

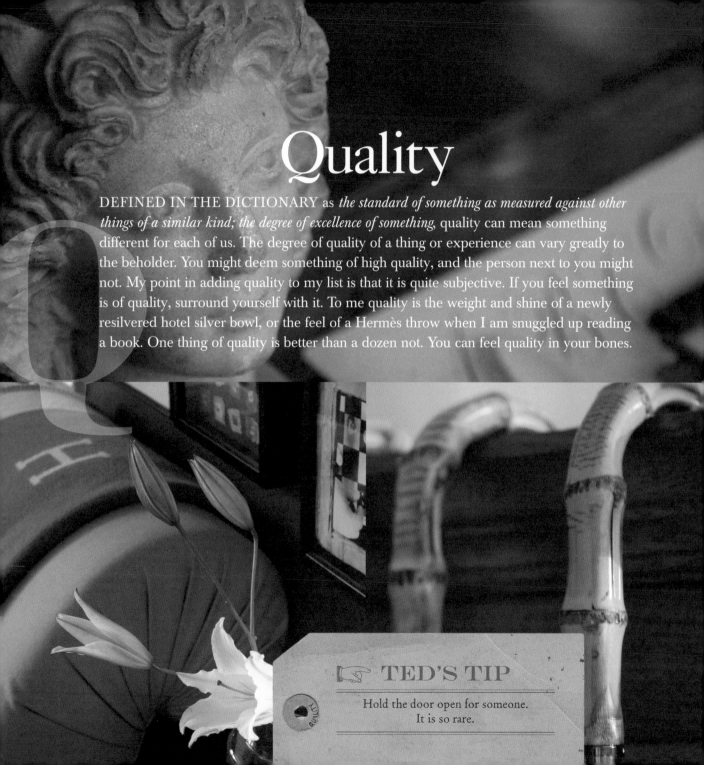

# Quality

DEFINED IN THE DICTIONARY as *the standard of something as measured against other things of a similar kind; the degree of excellence of something,* quality can mean something different for each of us. The degree of quality of a thing or experience can vary greatly to the beholder. You might deem something of high quality, and the person next to you might not. My point in adding quality to my list is that it is quite subjective. If you feel something is of quality, surround yourself with it. To me quality is the weight and shine of a newly resilvered hotel silver bowl, or the feel of a Hermès throw when I am snuggled up reading a book. One thing of quality is better than a dozen not. You can feel quality in your bones.

☞ TED'S TIP

Hold the door open for someone.
It is so rare.

*Risotto is one of those dishes that, once you master it, you will go back to time and again. It is both hearty and comforting either for a solo dinner or a crowd. The following recipe is the most basic. Start with it and then add what you like. Here are a few of my favorite things to add: sausage with butternut squash, a variety of wild mushrooms, shrimp and peas. A pinch of saffron adds a lovely complexity of flavor to risotto.*

## RISOTTO

1  Warm 7 cups of chicken stock in a pot on the stove, keeping it hot and at the ready.
2  In a good-size pot, such as a Le Creuset, sauté 1 finely chopped sweet onion in 4 tablespoons of extra virgin olive oil and a pat of butter.
3  Add 2 cups of Arborio rice and stir until evenly coated and hot.
4  Add 1 cup of white wine and simmer until absorbed.
5  Begin adding the hot chicken stock 1 cup at a time to the rice mixture, stirring frequently so the rice doesn't stick or burn (you want the rice at a brisk simmer).
6  When the liquid is absorbed, add another 1 cup, repeating until you have used 6 cups of the chicken stock. (This should take anywhere from 20 to 25 minutes.)
7  Season with salt, pepper, and 1 cup of freshly grated Parmigiano-Reggiano cheese.
8  Remove from heat, add a ½ cup of chicken stock, stir, and then let rest for a few minutes.
9  Once done, if you think it needs a bit more liquid so it's nice and creamy, add your remaining ½ of a cup of stock, stir, top with more cheese, and serve.

121

# Radishes

A FEW YEARS BACK, a French friend hosted a dinner party in our honor when we were in Paris. We had problems finding a parking space—how not surprising in Paris—and arrived a tad late. All of the other guests were sitting around an oversize coffee table in the very chic living room. Our artistic friend is a master of mixing things, people, objects, and food. Everyone was drinking champagne out of flat-bottomed glasses that were quite simple but yet, oh, so stylish. At the center of the table was a platter. On it was a large grouping of radishes, a pot of butter, and a dish of sea salt; this was the pre-dinner snack. I was intrigued. I certainly had used salt when eating radishes, but butter?

Some folks were casually dipping the radishes in the butter and eating them between sips of bubbly. Others would dip them in butter and then sprinkle a few flecks of sea salt over the radishes, salting the butter in the process. I tried it . . . and it was sublime! The bitterness of the radish mixed with the sweetness of the butter and the sting of the salt. It has now become a go-to snack to serve when I find a beautiful bunch of radishes and we have guests over. Give it a try. I hope you like it.

 **TED'S TIP**

Be ever present at your gathering.
This is not the time to be in the
kitchen cleaning up.

# Roasting Vegetables

ROASTING VEGETABLES ON A HIGH HEAT in the oven will make anyone a convert to liking almost any vegetable. It brings out the natural sweetness. I learned this from Ina Garten, the Barefoot Contessa. Take whatever vegetables you like—cauliflower, Brussels sprouts, onions, butternut squash, asparagus— coat them in extra virgin olive oil, and lay them on a sheet pan. Sprinkle with salt and pepper. Roast in a 400-degree oven, shaking the pan occasionally to ensure even cooking. Times vary per vegetable, so keep an eye on them. Sooooo good!

I DID BUSINESS WITH A FRENCH GENTLEMAN many years ago when I had my wholesale showroom. We were having a business dinner at a French restaurant, and he ordered a bottle of rosé. This was about fifteen years ago, and there was only one option on the wine list. It was quite a nice French restaurant, but back then rosé had not quite caught on. Now, there are many vintners offering rosé, which I love seeing. The gentleman said he grew up outside of Marseilles, and that his mother drank delicious pink wine year-round, always quite cold, and always with an ice cube added. I have been a fan ever since. Rosé speaks of summer and lazy afternoons. Try it year-round, though, when you want a nice fresh wine with your meal. Domaine Tempier and AIX are two of my very favorites. Veuve Clicquot also does a lovely rosé champagne that is out of this world. Drink pink!

{ *Life itself is the most wonderful fairy tale.* }

—Hans C. Anderson

# Rosemary

ROSEMARY IS ONE OF THOSE HERBS I reach for time and time again. Layer sprigs under a chicken and then roast it in the oven. The entire house will be filled with the luscious and earthy scent. I also love to add sprigs of rosemary to a bouquet of flowers, like zinnias or roses. The hearty stems play nicely off the blooms of the flowers. Rosemary is the first herb we choose each year when we replant our herb box out on the island. The heartiness of the plant makes it an easy-growing herb. The aromatic evergreen works nicely with a variety of other herbs.

# Rubber Stamps

WHERE WOULD WE BE WITHOUT RUBBER STAMPS! I use them practically every day at my shops to make a quick sign or to address an envelope. Rubber stamps come in a huge variety of sizes and designs, so finding sets that work for your needs can be quite easy. Choose an assortment of ink-pad colors so that you have lots of options to play with. If you are just beginning, try an alphabet set to get started. You will be amazed at how many projects you can incorporate the lettered rubber stamps into. Use them to make tags for gifts, personalize bookmarks, or stamp out a special card to a friend. I think of having a lettered rubber-stamp set around as like having a typewriter at the ready. They make it easy to quickly stamp out a sign or a quick note that looks quite professional. Try rubber stamping on vellum for a fun vintage look.

R

# Ribbon

RIBBON CAN COMPLETELY CHANGE THE LOOK OF A GIFT. Sure, great wrapping paper is a must, but the "just right" ribbon will elevate the entire presentation and overall excitement when the recipient is opening a gift. Good ribbon is fun. Look for it when you are out browsing at shops such as mine, or when you are at craft stores or fabric stores. Most retailers sell ribbon by the yard, so start a little ribbon box that you can add to, for when you are in a gift-wrapping mode. Buy whole rolls if the chosen ribbon just rocks your world. A well-wrapped gift is such a pretty thing.

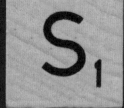

# Salon Style

HANGING YOUR ARTWORK "salon style" is by no means a new thing, but in recent years we are seeing it done more and more. It is a style I adore, as it instantly creates a warmth and sophistication in any room or home. The idea really is to create a collective whole, so that the eye sees the entire collection as one, but then sees each piece as individual. You are striving for balance. Hang some pieces closer together, others farther apart. Play around on the floor with the artwork first, moving things around until it pleases you. Then re-create it on your wall. My advice about hanging any art: you, the owner, must like it. Period. You are living with it each day. Keep moving it around until it makes your heart sing. Then you are done.

THE SINGLE-STEM VASE TRANSFORMED how I live with flowers many years back. The real joy of a flower is to look at it and examine each stem and bloom. The beauty of a single-stem vase is you get to do just that—to see each flower individually. It allows you to deck your space with multiple blooms while not breaking the bank in the process. Most grocery stores now have flower sections with buckets of flowers. A single-stem vase allows you to buy one, or a few, bunches and really get some flower impact for your home or dining table. I like to use clear vintage bottles we find on trips, but any type of receptacle will do: drinking glasses, Mason jars, or apothecary bottles. Change the water frequently and give the blooms a fresh cut, which will prolong the life and, ultimately, your enjoyment. Live with fresh flowers every day!

# Single-Stem Vase

# Silverware

SILVERWARE IS A WEAKNESS OF MINE. Rarely have I met a mother-of-pearl knife I didn't like or wouldn't work beautifully to serve cheese at dinner. Collecting silverware goes hand in hand with collecting dishes. Of course, it does not have to, but if you are at the antique mall, you might as well check out both. A mix-and-match table setting can look quite fetching. It highlights a collection. Have fun with the hunt. Look for serving pieces, as well. Whether horn, bone, sterling silver, silver plate, or mother-of-pearl, all can be components of beautiful silverware.

THINK STACKS OF BOOKS and stacks of magazines for starters. This goes hand in hand with **Multiples of Things** earlier. An unorganized scattering of books can look pretty fetching and camera ready when neatly stacked together, as do piles of blankets or piles of napkins. Everything is improved when rounded up and stacked together. Even if they are all different colors and textures, the mere fact of items collected and stacked together makes them a collective whole, which can be quite pleasing to the eye. It can also do wonders when trying to tidy up a mess.

131

# Stacks of Things

*Making homemade chicken stock is one of those tasks that is super easy, and the result is so completely satisfying. I like to do this on an evening after we roast a **Chicken** in the oven for dinner, and then use the carcass and any leftover meat still on the bone. Freeze what you are not going to use in the next several days and refrigerate what you will want right away. I love making **Risotto** with the fresh stock on the next night.*

## CHICKEN STOCK

1 Fill a good-size pot with water and add the cooked chicken carcass.
2 Add 2 white onions cut in half, several stalks of celery, a few unpeeled carrots, parsley still on the stems, 1 tablespoon of salt, and 12 peppercorns. There should be enough water to cover everything.
3 Bring to a boil, then reduce heat to a light simmer.
4 Simmer for 4 hours.
5 Take pot off heat to cool and then strain.

# Stock

# Seasonal Living

LIVING WITH THE SEASONS is as much an attitude as it is a daily practice. By living seasonally, you become much more aware of your surroundings, more present in the moment. Buy tulips at the beginning of spring, savor fresh corn and tomatoes in the summer, restock the wood pile in autumn, and plant paperwhite narcissus bulbs in a glass container in the winter. Actually, you can do all of these activities almost any time of the year, but doing them in their season means getting healthier tulips, eating better produce, and spending less on things that are in season. Seasonal living varies greatly with where you reside, but it really does enhance your daily experiences wherever you live.

*The principal thing in this world is to keep one's soul aloft.*
—*Gustave Flaubert*

# Seashells

ADDING A LITTLE BEACH TO A HOME can always be a bit of a pick-me-up for a room. It might be because I grew up in the Midwest, and since being by the water was a rarity, shells have always held a huge fascination for me. Seashells add a casualness to a setting. A bowl or clear glass hurricane filled with shells collected over time is such a lovely remembrance of past beach trips and outings. Or, take your favorite starfish and prop it up on a windowsill as a reminder of a relaxing day at the beach.

TULIPS SPEAK OF SPRING. When pressed, they are my very favorite flower. Tulips are a hearty flower which works beautifully with other blooms. I like them best when they are all bunched together and are the same color. They also have graceful leaves. Tulips are widely grown in hothouses and readily available in many grocery stores and markets. You can find them popping up in late winter, giving us the tulip season for an extended amount of time. Change the water every other day, and give the stems a fresh cut. This will prolong your enjoyment of the oh-so-lovely tulip.

THERE'S NOTHING LIKE TRAVEL to gain inspiration on many levels. It's a fabulous way to gain perspective; it makes us slow down a bit, allowing us to see all the beauty swirling around us. For many years now, I have had a blank moleskin journal that I take with me on each trip. It's not so much a journal that I write in each day of the trip with my thoughts—although I do occasionally do that—but rather it is for making notes on favorite restaurants and shops encountered, or jotting down the telephone number of a place to stay. All these things could be done on a phone or iPad, but I like that it becomes a physical remembrance of the trip. If it is not completely full, I take it on the next trip we make to that city. It's handy to have it easily accessible after trips for when a friend asks for a great spot for lunch in Rome, or the name of that little shop in Santa Barbara. The travel journals become a resource guide for your memories of a trip, to be enjoyed by you and others. It's also a fun spot to tape **Ephemera** that you collect along the way.

# Travel Journals

## ☞ TED'S TIP

Store your old travel journals in an easily accessible spot. They are so fun to refer back to when you are feeling an itch to take a trip. Like taking a sojourn without leaving your comfy chair.

# Throw Blankets

THERE IS SOMETHING ABOUT A STACK OF THROW BLANKETS that makes us want to curl up and read a good book. Draped over the back of a chair or laid across the foot of a bed, a throw blanket evokes warmth and hospitality. Whether it's cotton, wool, or cashmere, just make sure it launders easily, and your guests, and you, will reach for a throw blanket time and time again. A stack of throw blankets is a welcome addition to any guest room.

SETTING THE TABLE is one of my very favorite tasks when guests are coming over for a meal. It is also one of those tasks—I have learned from my customers—that can bring about quite a bit of stress. My point is to have fun with it. Who cares if everything doesn't match? Mixing and matching can make for a visually stunning table. Get creative. Use a tablecloth—don't use a tablecloth. Keep the flowers low, use lots of candles (votives are my go-to), and serve water with the meal (sparkling is always our choice). Mix in a few unexpected objects on the table. If you just got back from a trip, add a favorite memento to the tableau—it will make for a great conversation starter to the meal. Even if you are ordering pizza, set a stunning table. Celebrate the ordinary and make it extraordinary. If you make the table personal, it will just sing.

# Table Settings

# Tomatoes

A TOMATO SANDWICH, that is. When I was a kid, I was made these daily when I was at a tennis training camp in Kentucky. It is a sandwich with only four ingredients—if you count the sea salt—so it is key that each ingredient be the best you can find. Any good sourdough bread will work great for this sandwich. Just lightly toast the bread, which helps to keep the entire concoction from turning into a soggy mess. Next, and this is where you need to become friends with mayonnaise, you slather a good amount of it on both slices of the toasted bread. We have lots of friends who get queasy over excess mayo, but it is a must on this! After your first bite, you will understand why. Next, choose the ripest, juiciest tomato you can find. The juices combine with the mayo and make a sort of sauce. Slice the tomato quite thick. I think this sandwich is best served as open-faced. Add two slices of the tomato to the bread, side by side. Next, add a generous amount of French sea salt to the tops of the tomatoes. This will help draw out those delicious juices that we are hoping for. Let all sit for a minute or two, and then devour. They really are the yummiest darn things.

## ☞ TED'S TIP

Tomatoes make great flower "substitutes" if you are not finding blooms to your liking. Scatter tomatoes about your table. Fill clear glasses with cherry tomatoes. The color variations will make for a stellar and clever table setting.

NOTHING MAKES A TABLE SETTING SING quite like lovely utensils. If you are going to collect one culinary group, my advice would be to collect sets of flatware. They can often be picked up for a song at estate sales and antique malls. If you have a set of all-white dinnerware, you can switch it up by alternating utensil sets, making for creative table settings. House the different sets in glass containers, standing them upright so you can see the handles. It's a fun way to enjoy your collection when not in use.

Utensils

# Unpolished Silver

NOTHING BEATS THE LOOK OF POLISHED SILVER, but if it comes down to enjoying your silver or having it stored away in a closet, opt for unpolished silver any day. It has the preppy, Old World look I adore. An unpolished tray filled with candles or a grouping of tarnished vintage trophies all make me swoon. If you have it, have it out—use it, and enjoy it! So much of it has a history, a story. Seriously, have that gorgeous old stuff out and about. You will be happy you do.

# Vinaigrette

*Many Sunday mornings, I like to make some sort of egg breakfast, and often I will make a simple green salad to have with it. One of my favorite dressings I'll make is a simple shallot vinaigrette made with rice wine vinegar. Soaking the finely chopped shallot in the rice wine vinegar for a bit really mellows the bite that can come from the shallots. I usually start this process first, before I start anything else for the breakfast, so this combo can sit for a while. Of course, this vinaigrette is tasty at any meal, not just breakfast!*

## SHALLOT VINAIGRETTE

1  In a bowl, add 2 tablespoons of rice wine vinegar to 1 tablespoon of finely chopped shallot.
2  Add 1 teaspoon of Dijon mustard, with two good pinches of salt and one pinch of pepper.
3  Slowly mix in 6 tablespoons of extra virgin olive oil, whisking along the way. Let sit while you make the rest of the breakfast. Dress greens right before you are ready to eat. (Arugula is a particular favorite of mine.)

# Vintage

EVEN IF YOU ARE INTO MODERN INTERIORS, a little mix of vintage is always a welcome treat. Vintage goods add soul to a room. Vintage candlesticks, decanters, silver trays, bottles, artwork, ephemera—you name it. Whether handed down from your family or scored at a flea market on a memorable trip, vintage things will add a patina to your home, big or small. If you have inherited vintage goods such as stemware, use them! They are such a special daily reminder of the loved one who wanted you to have them. Here is a small project I play around with often at home and at my shops. Using pages from vintage books you can find at flea markets, tag sales, or library book sales can transform a wall or bookcase. It's a quick and easy project to use beautiful pages from vintage books that are falling apart—recycling at its finest!

1 First, make a stack of pages that speak to you, whether it's the images on the pages, the font, or the text. Try to use several different books so the size, color, and patina are varied.

2 Using double-sided tape, tape all four sides of the back of the page, making sure the side you like best is face up.

3 Start layering the sheets onto the wall, overlapping pages and filling in the desired space. In a pinch, you can use pushpins for a short-term display. The result will give visual interest and be a sort of wallpaper.

LET'S THINK OUTSIDE THE BOX on the standard definition of vases. A vase is anything you think works for holding blooms—simple drinking glasses, decorative pitchers, or vintage silver trophies. They all work divinely for holding flowers. Oftentimes, the vase can be as interesting to the setup as the flowers it is holding. So choose wisely, choose creatively, and you will be rewarded with one nifty-looking arrangement from top to bottom.

# Vases

# Wrapping

A WELL-WRAPPED GIFT can delight the recipient just as much as what is inside the box. A few added embellishments to make a package special and personalized really show you added extra care and thought to your gift. When out and about shopping, look for objects that have letters or numbers on them, such as vintage brass stencils, playing cards with letters on them, and buttons. I do not always have a recipient in mind, but I never pass up a card or other item that has a 30, 40, or 50 on it. The same goes for wrapping paper and ribbon. If I spot an interesting design, I get it and hold onto it until just the right occasion. If you can find a little spot in a closet or an armoire where you can keep wrapping supplies found along the way, you will look forward to wrapping your next gift. So often the stress of wrapping a gift lies in the lack of supplies—this will help alleviate that stress. Happy wrapping!

# White Bowls

WHITE BOWLS WORK IN BOTH VINTAGE AND MODERN INTERIORS. The reason I am concentrating just on white bowls is that lately there is a profusion of them out there in the marketplace. They make food look great, as it tends to pop and look more attractive in a white bowl or on a white platter. Bowls stack nicely, so you can have an ample number of them without taking up a lot of room. White bowls are also super party-friendly, working perfectly on a dining table or a buffet.

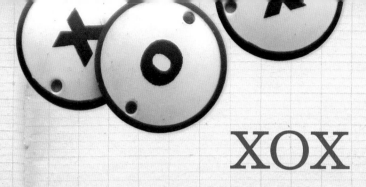

# XOX

MY DAD ALWAYS SIGNED CARDS to my mom with *XOX*. One of my earliest memories is asking him what it meant. To this day, I find it such a sweet way to end a note before my signature. The use of the *X* to signify a kiss dates back to medieval times, when a letter would actually be kissed to mean sincerity and honesty where the *X*, or cross, was placed.

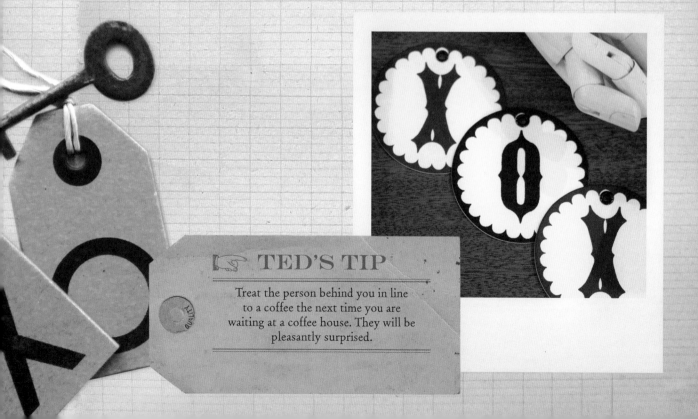

## ☞ TED'S TIP

Treat the person behind you in line to a coffee the next time you are waiting at a coffee house. They will be pleasantly surprised.

# Yellow

IN HERALDRY, yellow indicates honor and loyalty. Today, a yellow-painted wall or room is just happy. My office and our master bedroom are both painted a vibrant yellow. In fact, our favorite hotel in Paris, Hôtel le Tourville, has an all-yellow room that is our favorite room to stay in. Use this color to lift your spirits and mood. It's a perfect hue to use for a room that does not get much light, or when you just want to smile each time you enter the space. My favorite yellow is Benjamin Moore: Sun Kissed Yellow 2022-20.

{ *Yellow is capable of charming God.* }
—*Vincent van Gogh*

152

# Zinnias

ZINNIAS ARE SUCH PRETTY, PRETTY FLOWERS. They are among the few flowers I like to mix to have a variety of colors in a bunch. Abundant in the hot months, zinnias work swimmingly well with sprigs of herbs such as rosemary stems mixed about. If you change the water often and give the stems a fresh cut, your zinnias will last for a good long while for much enjoyment. For a colorful table display, gather some same-hued stems in a small vase at each place setting, using a different color for each vase. The table will be a riot of color, yet not overwhelming, as each setting's container is filled with blooms that are all the same color.

{ *I am going to make everything around me beautiful. That will be my life.* }

—*Elsie de Wolfe*

# Acknowledgments

WRITING AND PHOTOGRAPHING FOR THIS BOOK has been such a phenomenal process—a journey, really. I thank all of you who gave me encouragement along the way. To TPS, for being my biggest cheerleader and supporter, always. We live such a creative life together, with so many of the things on my list done as a duo. To our pooch, Bailey, for keeping me company as I worked away writing and photographing—she was always right by my side. Big thanks to my Watson Kennedy family, who kept the ship on course when I was away working on these pages, as well as for all the help in so many ways on these pages. To my editor at Sterling, John Foster, for your guidance and encouragement along the way. To Pamela Horn, who first read my blog and later my book proposal and said I had a "magical sensibility," and who worked with me on the initial A to Z concept. To the uber-creative graphic designer, Brent Whiting, who worked with me on the page designs and cover—such fun we had! *Merci* to my friend Barbara Barry for writing the foreword. We share a love of beauty, and I am so honored that you shared your words and insight. To Newell Turner, Anna Post, Lisa Birnbach, and Rita Konig, for your nice quotes—so, so incredibly kind of you all, and it meant the world to me. And, lastly, to all the customers, blog readers, and Instagram, Facebook, and Twitter followers who shop, buy, read, comment, and enjoy what I do, I feel so fortunate that I get to do what I do every day. Thank you, all, for joining me on this book journey.

— *XOX, Ted*

# Resources & Inspiration

LOCAL INDEPENDENT RETAILERS are always my first choice when shopping, as they provide towns and cities their personalities and flavors. The following are some of my favorite places to shop. These merchants have inspired me over the years, some have become friends, and all offer amazing wares year in and year out. We have filled our homes with beautiful things we enjoy each and every day from:

*ABC Carpet & Home* (New York), *Aero* (New York), *Bellocchio* (San Francisco), *Bergdorf Goodman* (New York), *Bountiful* (Santa Monica), *Dempsey & Carroll* (New York), *de Vera* (New York), *John Derian* (New York), *Sue Fisher King* (San Francisco), *Tale of the Yak* (Berkeley), and *Treillage* (New York).

## WEBSITES

Anthropologie (for house & home goods)

CB2 (for Marta glassware and trays)

eBay (for vintage)

Etsy (for one-of-a-kind handmade goods)

Gumps (for accessories)

Hermes (for blankets)

L.L.Bean (for preppy standards)

One Kings Lane (for their unique daily tastemaker sales)

Orvis (for outdoorsy goods)

Ralph Lauren (for bedding and towels)

Sur la Table (for kitchenware)

Target (for designer collaboration goods)

Terrain (for cool garden stuff)

Williams Sonoma (for kitchenware)

## INSPIRATIONAL PUBLICATIONS

*Anthology; Country Living; Domino; Elle Décor; Food & Wine; Garden and Gun; Gather; House Beautiful; Kinfolk; Lonny; Martha Stewart Living; Matchbook; The New York Times* (T Magazine, Home, Style, and Food sections); *Rue; Saveur; Town & Country; Vanity Fair; Veranda; Vogue; Wall Street Journal* (Saturday Off Duty section)

## PEOPLE, PLACES, AND GOODS I LIKE, LOVE, AND ADORE

This list changes often. Check my daily blog at www.TedKennedyWatson.com for updates.

Axel Vervoordt; Barbara Barry; Boat Street Cafe; Brian Paquette; Bunny Williams; Buvette; Cafe Campagne; Cafe Presse; Canal House; Coco + Kelley; David Lebovitz; Dean & DeLuca; Dempsey & Carroll; Eddie Ross; For the Love of a House; Grant K. Gibson; Gwyneth Paltrow; Habitually Chic; Ina Garten; Jon Call; Matt's in the Market; My Notting Hill; Not Without Salt; Orangette; Pretty Pink Tulips; Prune; Rita Konig; Rural Intelligence; Sacramento Street; Smitten Kitchen; Spinasse; Style Saloniste; Unabashedly Prep; Veuve Clicquot; and Zuni Cafe

# Index